SPANISH
GCSE REVISION

TECHNOLOGY & MEDIA
SOCIAL ISSUES

THE LANGUAGE GYM

Imprint Independently Published

Edited by Roberto Jover Soro, Inés Głowacka & Paloma Lozano García

THE LANGUAGE GYM

DEDICATION

For Catrina

- Gianfranco

For Mariana

- Ronan

For Ariella and Leonard

- Dylan

ACKNOWLEDGEMENTS

Our heartfelt thanks to our team of guest proofreaders: Marta Bernard, Ester Borin, Ana del Casar, Chris Pye, Sonja Fedrizzi, Jaume Llorens & Leticia Veiga. Their contributions have ensured not only a highly accurate book but also helped make some improvements in terms of choice of lexis. Thank you for your lending your time and expertise to this project.

Our gratitude to Martin Lapworth for his time spent creating online versions of the Sentence Builders contained in this book. These are now available, via subscription, on SentenceBuilders.com. The feedback given by Martin not only on the final draft, but throughout the process, was instrumental in making some key content decisions and tweaks. Thank you.

Big thanks to my students, Marc Tang, Sam Sajan & Joshua Tomson for their helpful and intuitive suggestions. These have helped improve the overall useability of the book.

Lastly, thanks to all the wonderful, supportive and passionate educators on Twitter who have helped enhance our book with their suggestions and comments, and to the members of the Global Innovative Language Teachers (GILT) Facebook group for their engagement with the Sentence Builders series. We consider ourselves very lucky to have such colleagues to inspire and spur us on.

ABOUT THIS BOOK

Welcome,

If you're reading this, it means you've either bought, or are contemplating buying this book.

Either way, thank you.

As with all Language Gym books, our small team has gone to great efforts to produce a high-quality, affordable, no frills resource. Feedback from the three international and three UK-based schools on the content of this book has been overwhelmingly positive. As with our previous publications, the evidence shows that the E.P.I. method really does produce excellent results. As full-time teachers who use these resources across all levels they teach, Ronan and Dylan can also vouch for the method first-hand. We know that the care taken throughout the creation process will reflect in the quality of the resource and do hope that you and your students enjoy using it!

This book is meant as a revision resource for GCSE Spanish. It can be used independently by students as well as for teacher-directed classroom practice. It contains 8 units which focus mainly on the themes *technology, media and social issues.*

Each unit consists of a knowledge organiser recapping the target sentence patterns and lexical items, a series of receptive vocab-building activities; a set of narrow reading texts and activities; a set of translation tasks. The tasks are graded in order to pose an increasingly demanding but manageable cognitive load and challenge and are based on Dr Conti's P.I.P.O. framework

Pre-reading tasks (activation of prior knowledge and pre-teaching)

In-reading tasks (intensive exploitation of tasks)

Post-reading tasks (consolidation)

Output (pushed-output tasks)

Consistent with Dr Conti's E.P.I. approach, each of the 8 units in the book provide extensive recycling of the target lexical items both within each unit and throughout the book, across all the dimensions of receptive and productive processing, i.e. orthography (single letters and syllables), lexis (both words and chunks), grammar/syntax (with much emphasis on functional and positional processing), meaning and discourse. The recycling occurs through input-flooding and forced retrieval through a wide range of engaging, tried and tested, classic Conti tasks (more than 20 per unit). These include student favourites such as slalom writing, faulty translation, spot the missing detail, sentence puzzles, etc.

Thanks,

Gianfranco, Ronan & Dylan

TABLE OF CONTENTS

Unit 1. Technology in everyday life

Cada mañana *Every morning*	me despierto *I wake up*	con la alarma del móvil *with my mobile phone alarm*

Casi siempre *Almost always* Normalmente *Usually* Por lo general *Generally*	me divierto *I have fun* me relajo *I relax* paso mi tiempo *I spend my time*	chateando con mis amigos *chatting (online) with my friends* escribiendo mensajes en WhatsApp *writing messages on WhatsApp* haciendo crucigramas en línea *doing online crosswords* leyendo las noticias en mi tablet *reading the news on my tablet* viendo vídeos en YouTube *watching videos on YouTube*

o	como cereales *I eat some cereals* tomo el desayuno *I have breakfast*	mientras *while*	entro en mi Instagram *I go on my Instagram* leo las noticias *I read the news* veo vídeos *I watch videos*

Entre semana *During the week*	me meto en internet *I go on the internet* uso mi ordenador *I use my computer*	para hacer mis deberes *to do my homework* para buscar información *to look for information*

A veces *Sometimes* Cuando tengo tiempo, *When I have the time,* De vez en cuando *From time to time* Si tengo tiempo, *If I have the time,*	descargo aplicaciones *I download apps*	de internet *from the internet*
	escucho música *I listen to music*	en Spotify *on Spotify*
	subo algunas fotos *I upload some photos*	a mi cuenta de Instagram *to my Instagram account* a mis redes sociales *to my social networks*
	veo series *I watch series*	en Netflix *on Netflix*

Antes de acostarme, *Before going to bed,* Cuando vuelvo del colegio, *When I come back from school,* Después de la cena, *After dinner,* Después de terminar las tareas, *After having finished my homework,* Después del colegio, *After school,* Por la tarde *In the evening*	chateo *I chat (online)* escribo un blog *I write a blog* hablo por Skype *I talk on Skype* hago mi trabajo escolar en línea *I do my schoolwork online* juego a videojuegos en línea *I play online video games* leo revistas digitales *I read digital magazines*	con mi familia *with my family* con mi hermano *with my brother* con mi hermana *with my sister* con mi mejor amigo/a *with my best friend* con mis compañeros de clase *with my classmates* solo/sola *on my own*

THE LANGUAGE GYM

1. Translate into English

a. Hago mi trabajo escolar en línea

b. Escribo un blog

c. Descargo aplicaciones

d. Me meto en internet

e. Subo algunas fotos

f. Leo revistas digitales

g. Juego a videojuegos en línea

h. Chateo con mi mejor amiga

i. Escribiendo mensajes en WhatsApp

j. Haciendo crucigramas en línea

k. Chateando con mis amigos

2. Match

En línea	Sometimes
Leo	Crosswords
Crucigramas	I write
Subo	I talk
Móvil	Online
Hablo	Digital
Descargo	I upload
Digital	I read
A veces	Mobile
Escribo	I download

3. Complete with the missing words

a. Chateo en _____   *I chat online*

b. _____ un blog   *I write a blog*

c. Me _____ en internet   *I go on the internet*

d. _____ aplicaciones   *I download apps*

e. Hago mi _____ escolar en línea   *I do my schoolwork online*

f. Juego a _____ en línea   *I play online video games*

g. Leo revistas _____   *I read digital magazines*

h. _____ algunas fotos   *I upload some photos*

i. _____ cereales   *I eat cereals*

j. _____ crucigramas en línea   *Doing online crosswords*

4. Complete the words

a. Des_____   *I download*

b. Ch_____   *I chat (online)*

c. D_____   *Digital*

d. L_____   *I read*

e. En lí_____   *Online*

f. Mó_____   *Mobile*

g. Es_____   *I listen*

h. A v_____   *Sometimes*

i. S_____   *I upload*

5. Sentence puzzle

a. el vídeos mientras en desayuno Tomo veo YouTube

   I have breakfast watching videos on YouTube

b. Como las mientras en noticias cereales tablet leo mi

   I eat cereals reading the news on my tablet

c. Me Netflix viendo relajo en series

   I relax watching series on Netflix

d. WhatsApp Paso tiempo mi mensajes en escribiendo

   I spend my time writing messages on WhatsApp

e. chateando mis con Me divierto amigos

   I have fun chatting (online) with my friends

6. Faulty translation: spot the wrong translations and correct them

Después de la cena *After breakfast*

Después de terminar las tareas
Before starting my homework

Después del colegio *After university*

Cuando vuelvo del colegio
When I come back from work

Antes de acostarme *After going to bed*

Por la tarde *In the morning*

Hago mi trabajo escolar en línea
I do my schoolwork on the computer

7. Spot and write the missing word. Note there is one missing word per sentence and it is always a very short one

a. Me divierto chateando mis amigos

b. Paso mi tiempo escribiendo mensajes WhatsApp

c. Antes acostarme leo revistas digitales

d. Cuando vuelvo colegio, juego a videojuegos en línea

e. Después la cena, hablo por Skype con mi primo Ronnie

f. Tomo desayuno mientras leo las noticias en mi tablet

g. Normalmente meto en internet para buscar información

h. Casi siempre hago trabajo escolar en línea

8. Likely or Unlikely?

a. Chateo con mi perro

b. Hago el trabajo escolar

c. Hablo al ordenador

d. Como fotos a Instagram

e. Juego a videojuegos

f. Leo antes de acostarme

g. Busco información en mi tablet

h. Tomo el desayuno chateando con mis cereales

9. Multiple-choice quiz

	1	2	3
I relax	Escribo	Me relajo	Hago
I have fun	Me aburro	Me divierto	Veo
I read	Subo	Juego	Leo
I have (eat)	Tomo	Hablo	Escucho
I talk	Hablo	Vuelvo	Me acuesto
I download	Tomo	Descargo	Me ducho
I wake up	Me divierto	Me relajo	Me despierto
I chat	Chatea	Chateo	Gateo

10. Gapped sentences

a. Nor_____ h_____ mi t_____ e_____ en _____

b. Por la n_____, antes de a_____, l_____ r_____ digitales

c. Cuando l_____ del colegio, juego a v_____ en línea

d. Por la mañana t_____ el desayuno mientras v_____ vídeos e____ YouTube

e. D_____ de la cena, h_____ por Skype con m_____ primo

f. Me r_____ j_____ a la Play

g. Me d_____ con la a_____ de mi _____

h. Por la t_____ veo s_____ en línea con mis hermanos

i. Tomo el d_____ m_____ l_____ las noticias _____ mi tablet

TEXT 1 – Javi (16 años, San Roque)

(1) Cada mañana me despierto con la alarma de mi móvil. Es práctico porque no tengo que comprar un despertador. Normalmente desayuno mientras leo las noticias en mi tablet o hago crucigramas en línea. Me gusta mucho Wordle porque aprendo palabras nuevas todos los días. A veces también como cereales mientras veo vídeos en YouTube o escribo mensajes en WhatsApp, depende de mi estado de ánimo.

(2) Entre semana uso mi ordenador para hacer mis tareas y me conecto a internet para buscar información. Suelo pasar unas tres horas al día en internet durante la semana. Durante el fin de semana suelo pasar aún más tiempo en internet, porque escucho música en Spotify o veo series en Netflix. El fin de semana pasado hice un maratón de Netflix con mi mejor amigo y ¡fue increíble! Cuando tengo tiempo, subo vídeos a mi cuenta de YouTube y también subo fotos a mi Instagram.

(3) Cuando llego a casa después del colegio, hago mi trabajo escolar en línea con mis compañeros de clase. Después de terminar mis tareas, si tengo tiempo, juego a videojuegos en línea con mi hermano mayor. Nos encantan especialmente los juegos de guerra. Después de la cena, a menudo hablo por Skype con mis primos que viven en el extranjero. Viven en Australia, por lo que no siempre es fácil debido a la diferencia horaria.

(4) Antes de acostarme, escribo un blog o leo revistas digitales en mi dormitorio. Normalmente, entre semana, me acuesto a eso de las diez, y un poco más tarde los fines de semana porque no tengo que levantarme temprano a la mañana siguiente.

11. Find in the paragraph 1 of Javi's text

a. I wake up

b. My mobile phone

c. I don't need

d. Alarm clock

e. While reading

f. While doing

g. I learn new words

h. While writing

12. Answer the following questions in English about paragraphs 2 and 3

a. What does he use the computer for during the week?

b. When does he spend more time on the internet, during the week or at the weekend? Why?

c. Who did he watch a lot of Netflix last weekend with? How was it?

d. What does he do when he has the time?

e. What does he do on returning from school?

f. What does he do with his older brother?

g. What kind of games do they like?

h. Why is it not easy to chat with his cousins?

13. Complete the translation of paragraph 3 below

When I _____ after _____, I do my schoolwork _____ with my classmates. After _____, if _____, I play video games _____ with my _____ brother. We _____ like _____ games. After _____, I _____ talk on Skype with my cousins who live _____. They live in Australia, therefore it is not always _____ because of the _____.

14. True, False or Not mentioned?

a. Javi wakes up to his alarm clock

b. Javi has a younger brother

c. He does crosswords whilst having breakfast

d. He likes Wordle because it is fun, but he doesn't learn anything from it

e. He spends maximum three hours a day on the internet during the weekend

f. He binge-watched Netflix last weekend

g. After doing his homework he plays video games with his older brother

15. Try to complete this summary of Javi's text with the verbs in the table below

Todos los días, Javi se _____ con la alarma de su móvil. Luego, por lo general, _____ el desayuno mientras _____ las noticias en su tablet. Le gusta mucho Wordle porque a menudo _____ palabras nuevas. A veces come cereales mientras ve vídeos en YouTube o _____ mensajes a sus amigos en WhatsApp. Entre semana, _____ su ordenador para hacer sus tareas y se conecta a internet para _____ información. Durante el fin de semana _____ más tiempo en internet porque escucha música en Spotify o ve sus series favoritas en Netflix. Cuando tiene tiempo, sube vídeos y fotos a su cuenta de Instagram. Cuando llega a casa del colegio, _____ sus deberes en línea con sus compañeros de clase. Después, si tiene tiempo, juega a videojuegos en línea con su hermano. Prefieren los juegos de guerra. Después de _____ la cena, a menudo chatea por Skype con sus primos que _____ en Australia. Antes de _____, escribe un blog o _____ en su Instagram en su dormitorio. Normalmente se acuesta a eso de las diez _____ semana y un poco más tarde los fines de semana porque no tiene que levantarse temprano a la mañana siguiente.

buscar	toma	usa	lee	entra	escribe	acostarse
aprende	hace	despierta	viven	tomar	pasa	entre

---

16. Translate the following words/phrases from the text above (the first letter is given)

a. Every day: T

b. Digital: D

c. Online: E

d. Sometimes: A

e. Computer: O

f. New words: P

g. They prefer: P

h. He chats: C

i. Before going to bed: A

j. Usually: N

k. Alarm: A

l. He doesn't have to: N

---

17. Find in the text above the following words and translate them into English

a. A plural adjective starting with 'N'

b. A time adverb starting with 'A'

c. A verb starting with 'T'

d. A singular feminine noun starting with 'I'

e. A time adverb starting with 'N'

f. A verb starting with 'L'

g. A noun starting with 'C'

h. A plural feminine noun starting with 'R'

18. Translate into Spanish

a. Digital magazines

b. Mobile phone

c. I go on the internet

d. I do my homework online

e. Reading information on my tablet

f. Before going to bed

g. After having dinner

h. New words

TEXT 2 – Paloma (15 años, Granada)

(1) Entre semana me despierto a las seis y media con la alarma de mi móvil. A eso de las siete menos cuarto, bebo chocolate caliente y como cereales mientras hablo con mis amigos por mensajería instantánea. Me gusta tomarme mi tiempo por la mañana, así que siempre me levanto más temprano para no tener prisa. Normalmente, salgo de casa a eso de las ocho menos cuarto.

(2) Entre semana uso mi ordenador todos los días para hacer mis tareas por la tarde y también para jugar a videojuegos en línea con mis amigos por la noche. En la universidad, en la clase de informática, aprendo a usar programas como procesadores de textos *[word processors]* por ejemplo. Me gusta la informática porque es interesante y también muy práctica en la vida cotidiana. Creo que también es importante para encontrar un trabajo en el futuro porque estamos usando cada vez más las nuevas tecnologías y los ordenadores son las herramientas del futuro.

(3) Después del colegio, hago mi trabajo escolar en línea con mis compañeros de clase. Una vez que termino mis deberes, normalmente escucho música en Spotify o subo fotos a mi cuenta de Instagram. Sé que paso demasiado tiempo frente a la pantalla todos los días, y mis padres siempre me dicen que debería salir más de mi casa y hacer deportes al aire libre en lugar de malgastar mi tiempo jugando a la consola.

(4) Por la noche, chateo con mi mejor amiga o veo series en Netflix hasta las diez y media. Luego me lavo los dientes y me acuesto porque tengo que levantarme temprano al día siguiente para ir al colegio.

19. Find the Spanish equivalent in the first two paragraphs

a. During the week

b. While I talk

c. I like to take my time

d. So as not to rush

e. I use my computer

f. Video games

g. Everyday life

h. New technologies

i. The tools of the future

j. To find a job

20. Answer the questions below about the text

a. Why does Paloma wake up early in the morning?

b. What does she do at 7:45am?

c. Why does she like ICT (3 reasons)?

-

-

-

d. What does she do online with her classmates after school?

e. What do her parents criticise her for? What do they suggest she should do instead (2 details)?

-

-

21. Complete with the correct word with the help of the text

a. Me gusta _____ mi tiempo   *I like to take my time*

b. Cada vez _____   *More and more*

c. _____   *I chat (online)*

d. Las _____ tecnologías   *New technologies*

e. _____ mi consola   *On my games console*

f. Uso mi _____   *I use my computer*

g. Todos los _____   *Every day*

22. Match

Chateando	Tools
Cada día	Chatting
Noticias	Schoolwork
El trabajo escolar	To my account
A mi cuenta	News
Herramientas	Software
Programas	ICT
Informática	Daily

23. Sentence puzzle: rewrite the sentences in the correct order

a. días ordenador Uso mi los todos

b. Por mi la amigo chateo con noche mejor.

c. nuevas Utilizamos cada las más tecnologías vez

d. informática Me interesante gusta la es porque.

e. Me tomarme gusta mi por tiempo mañana la.

f. chateo Como instantánea mientras mensajería por.

g. demasiado Paso a tiempo pantalla frente la.

h. móvil Me con despierto la de alarma mi

24. Complete using the options provided below

Entre _____, todos los días, me _____ a las seis y media con la alarma del _____. Después, a las siete menos cuarto, _____ chocolate caliente y como cereales _____ chateo con mis amigos en mi _____. Me encanta _____ mi tiempo por las mañanas, por eso siempre me_____ temprano y así no _____ darme prisa. Normalmente, _____ de casa a las ocho menos cuarto.

tablet	mientras	bebo	despierto	tomarme
salgo	semana	levanto	móvil	tengo que

25. Complete the Spanish sentences

a. _____ mi ordenador *I use my computer*

b. Debería _____ más de mi casa
I should get out more of my house

c. _____ mi trabajo escolar _____
I do my schoolwork online

d. Me gusta la_____ porque es interesante
I like ICT because it is interesting

e. Leo revistas _____ en mi habitación
I read digital magazines in my bedroom

f. Por la tarde _____ series en Netflix
In the afternoon/evening I watch series on Netflix

g. _____ fotos a mi _____ de Instagram
I post photos on my Instagram account

26. Translate into Spanish

a. Download: D

b. Information: I

c. To chat: C

d. Online: E

e. Account: C

f. New technologies: N

g. Mobile phone: M

h. Video games: V

i. On my console: E

j. I spend my time: P

27. Complete with the missing words

a. Subo fotos _ mi cuenta de Instagram

b. Leo revistas digitales _ _ mi cuarto

c. Después _ _ terminar mis deberes juego _ videojuegos

d. Aprendo _ utilizar _ _ _ redes sociales

e. Paso mi _ _ _ _ _ _ escribiendo mensajes _ _ WhatsApp

f. Descubro canciones nuevas _ _ Spotify

g. Desayuno mientras chateo _ _ _ mis amigos

h. Me despierto _ _ _ _ seis _ _ _ la alarma _ _ mi móvil

i. Cuando vuelvo _ _ _ colegio escribo _ _ blog

28. Anagrams

a. sdeRe sealiocs	*Social networks*
b. mopTie	*Time*
c. Plantaal	*Screen*
d. Toféléfon limóv	*Mobile phone*
e. eRd	*Network*
f. sogeVijudeo	*Video games*
g. Canetu	*Account*
h. nE	*On*
i. deanOrdor	*Computer*

29. Translate into Spanish

a. After finishing my homework

b. After listening to music

c. After having breakfast

d. After playing vídeo games

e. After chatting with my best friend

f. After using my computer

g. After having dinner

30. Translate into Spanish

a. I post

b. I chat

c. I read

d. I use

e. I play

f. I watch

g. I listen to

h. I have fun

31. Guided translation

a. M_ d_____ a l___ s__ c__ l_ a_____ d_ m_____
I wake up at 6:00 to the alarm of my mobile

b. D_____ m_____ c_____ c__ m__ a_____
I have breakfast chatting with my friends

c. S____ f_____ a m__ c_____ d_ I_____
I post photos on my Instagram account

d. P_____ d_____ t___ d_____ d_ l_ p_____
I spend too much time in front of the screen

e. M__ d_____ j_____ e__ m__ t_____
I have fun playing on my tablet

f. D_____ s_____ m_ e_ v_ d_ p_____ e_ t____ j_____ a l__ v_____
I should go out more instead of wasting (losing) time playing video games

g. D_____ d_ t_____ m_ t_____ e_____ , c_____ c__ m_ a_____ e_ WhatsApp
After finishing my school work, I chat with my friends on WhatsApp

h. U__ m_ o_____ p____ b_____ i_____ e_ l__ r_____ d_____
I use my computer to look for information in digital magazines

32. Write a paragraph to translate Roberto's texts in the FIRST person singular (juego, hago) and another saying the same thing for Inés in the THIRD person singular (lee, desayuna, etc.)

ENGLISH	Roberto (first person) /Inés (third person)
e.g. I wake up to the alarm of my mobile phone at 6.	**Roberto:** Me despierto con la alarma de mi móvil a las seis. **Inés:** Se despierta con la alarma de su móvil a las seis.
I shower then I have breakfast with my brother.	
I have cereals with milk whilst chatting with my friends on WhatsApp.	
After breakfast, I shower, get dressed, and then brush my teeth listening to music on Spotify.	
I leave my home around 8:00	
At school I cannot use my mobile phone, but we use the tablet a lot in lessons.	
After school, I use my computer a lot to do my homework.	
In some subjects, I do the school work online with my friends.	
After finishing my homework, I play on PlayStation, post photos on Instagram or share funny videos on Facebook.	
Sometimes I use Skype to chat with my cousing who live in Australia.	
Before going to bed, I usually write my blog.	
Before falling asleep, I read digital magazines or watch series on Netflix.	

Key questions

¿Cómo utilizas las nuevas tecnologías en tu día a día?	*How do you use new technologies in your everyday life?*
¿Qué sueles hacer en tu ordenador?	*What do you do generally do on your computer?*
¿Cuál es tu videojuego favorito?	*Which is your favourite video game?*
¿Para qué usas internet normalmente?	*What do you normally use internet for?*
¿Te gustan las nuevas tecnologías? ¿Por qué?	*Do you like new technologies? Why?*
¿Tienes un teléfono móvil? ¿Desde cuándo?	*Do you have a mobile phone? Since when?*
¿Utilizas tu teléfono móvil para el ocio? ¿Cómo?	*Do you use your mobile phone for leisure? How?*
¿Tienes una tablet también?	*Do you also have a tablet?*
¿Cuánto tiempo sueles pasar en internet cada día?	*How much time do you generally spend on the internet per day?*
¿Prefieres hacer tus deberes con o sin internet? ¿Por qué?	*Do you prefer doing your homework with or without internet? Why?*
¿Crees que los jóvenes de hoy en día pasan demasiado tiempo frente a una pantalla? ¿Cuál es el peligro?	*Do you think that today's youngsters spend too much time in front of a screen? What is the danger?*

Unit 1. Technology in everyday life (past tense)

Ayer por la mañana *Yesterday morning*	**me desperté** *I woke up*	**con la alarma del móvil** *with my mobile phone's alarm*

A eso de las siete *Around 7am* **Después** *Afterwards* **Entonces** *Then* **Más tarde** *Shortly after*	**bebí un zumo de naranja** *I drank an orange juice* **comí una tostada** *I ate a piece of toast* **desayuné** *I had breakfast*	**mientras contestaba los mensajes** *while answering to my messages* **mientras hablaba con mis amigos/as** *while chatting with my friends* **mientras hacía un crucigrama en línea** *while doing an online crossword* **mientras jugaba a la PlayStation** *while playing on the PlayStation* **mientras leía las noticias en la tablet** *while reading the news on my tablet* **mientras veía vídeos en YouTube** *while watching videos on YouTube*

Hace dos días *Two days ago* **El lunes pasado** *Last Monday*	**usé mi ordenador** *I used my computer* **usé internet** *I went on the internet*	**para buscar información** *to look for information* **para editar un vídeo** *to edit a video*

Anteayer *The day before yesterday* **Ayer por la tarde** *Yesterday afternoon/evening* **La semana pasada** *Last week* **El miércoles por la tarde** *On Wednesday afternoon*	**escuché música** *I listened to music* **subí fotos** *I posted photos* **vi una película / serie** *I watched a film / series*	**en Spotify** *on Spotify* **a mi Instagram** *on my Instagram account* **en línea** *online* **en Netflix** *on Netflix*

Antes de acostarme, *Before going to bed,* **Cuando llegué del colegio,** *When I came back from school,* **Después de cenar,** *After having dinner,* **Después de hacer los deberes,** *After finishing my homework,* **Después del colegio,** *After school,* **Por la noche** *In the evening/night*	**chateé** *I chatted online* **hice un BeReal/TikTok** *I made a BeReal/TikTok* **hice una videollamada** *I made a video call* **hice los deberes en línea** *I did my homework online* **jugué a videojuegos en línea** *I played video games online* **leí las noticias en línea** *I read the news online*	**con mis amigos/as** *with my friends* **con mi hermana mayor** *with my big sister* **con mi hermano pequeño** *with my little brother* **con mi novio/a** *with my boyfriend/girlfriend* **con mi primo/a** *with my cousin* **solo/a** *on my own*

1. Match

Por la tarde	The day before yesterday
Ayer	Two days ago
Anteayer	Last week
Entonces	In the afternoon/evening
Antes de acostarme	Then
Cuando llegué	Yesterday afternoon/evening
Ayer por la tarde	Yesterday
La semana pasada	When I came back
Hace dos días	Before going to bed

2. Complete

a. Un _____ *A crossword*

b. Los _____ *Video games*

c. Los _____ *Homework*

d. La _____ *Videocall*

e. En _____ *Online*

f. _____ *On my own (fem)*

g. El _____ *Mobile phone*

h. Mi _____ *My account*

3. Complete with the missing verb forms

a. Anteayer _____ una videollamada con mi hermana mayor

b. El miércoles por la mañana _____ las noticias en línea

c. Antes de acostarme _____ música en mi habitación

d. Ayer _____ a videojuegos en línea

e. La semana pasada _____ una serie en Netflix

f. A eso de las siete _____ cereales con leche mientras _____ un crucigrama

g. Anteayer _____ internet para _____ información

h. Ayer por la tarde _____ un BeReal con mi móvil

4. Complete the table with the past (preterite) tense forms (*yo*)

Present	Past tense
Juego	
Bebo	
Tomo	
Escribo	
Como	
Hablo	
Subo	
Chateo	

5. Break the flow then translate into English

a. Juguéavideojuegosenlínea

b. Desayunéhaciendocrucigramasenlínea

c. ViunaserieenNetflix

d. BebíunchocolatecalientemientraschateabaporWhatsApp

e. Desayunécerealesmientrasleíalasnoticiasenmimóvil

f. Uséinternetparabuscarinformación

g. DesayunéunatostadamientrasveíavídeosenYouTube

h. BebíuncafémientrascontestabalosmensajesenTwitter

i. ComímientrasjugabaenmiPlayStation

j. HabléconmiamigomientrasescuchabamúsicaenSpotify

TEXT 1 – Manu (15 años, Santa Cruz del Comercio)

Ayer por la mañana me desperté temprano con la alarma de mi móvil. ¡Es conveniente porque no tengo que comprar un despertador! Luego, bebí leche caliente mientras leía las noticias en mi tablet y hacía crucigramas en línea. Me gusta mucho Spotify porque escucho mi música favorita todos los días. Después, comí huevos con jamón mientras veía vídeos en YouTube y respondía a mis mensajes.

El lunes pasado usé mi ordenador para hacer mis deberes y me metí en internet para buscar información. Paso una media de tres horas al día en internet durante la semana, ¡pero ayer pasé seis horas! Durante el fin de semana suelo pasar aún más tiempo en internet porque escucho música en Spotify o veo series en Netflix. El fin de semana pasado hice un maratón de películas en Netflix con mi mejor amigo y ¡fue realmente increíble! Además, tuve tiempo de leer noticias y también subí fotos nuevas a mi cuenta de Instagram.

Cuando llegué del colegio, hice mis deberes en línea junto con mis compañeros de clase. Después de terminar mis deberes, jugué a videojuegos en línea con mi hermano mayor. Nos gustan especialmente los juegos de guerra. Después de cenar, hice una videollamada con mis primos que viven en el extranjero. Viven en Australia, por lo que no siempre es fácil encontrar un buen momento para hablar por la diferencia horaria entre España y Australia.

Antes de acostarme, escribí un comentario en Instagram y busqué un poco de información con mi tablet. Normalmente me acuesto alrededor de las diez durante la semana, pero ayer me acosté un poco antes porque estaba muy cansado.

6. Find the Spanish equivalent in the text

a. I woke up early

b. I drank hot milk

c. I ate eggs

d. I used my computer

e. I went on the internet

f. I spent six (hours)

g. I did a movie marathon

h. It was really great

i. I had time

j. I came back from school

k. I made a videocall

l. The time difference

7. The sentences below have been copied incorrectly from the text. Correct them

a. Me desperté tarde con la alarma

b. Bebí leche fría mientras leía las noticias

c. Usé mi ordenador para hacer mis mensajes

d. Hago un maratón de películas en Netflix

e. Después de cenar hacía una videollamada

f. Busqué un poco de información en mi móvil

g. Me acuesto un poco antes porque estaba muy cansado

8. Complete the sentences below based on Manu's text

a. Yesterday morning, Manu drank _____ while _____

b. He likes Spotify _____ because he _____

c. He ate _____ while watching YouTube and _____

d. On average he _____ on the internet during the week

e. Last weekend he did a Netflix marathon with _____

f. When he came back from school he did _____

TEXT 2 – María (17 años, Badajoz)

El viernes por la mañana me desperté a las seis y media con la alarma de mi móvil. Alrededor de las siete menos cuarto, bebí zumo de manzana y comí una tostada con tomate mientras chateaba con mis amigos por WhatsApp. Me gusta tomarme mi tiempo por la mañana, así que siempre me levanto más temprano para no tener prisa. Luego salí de casa alrededor de las ocho menos cuarto.

Durante el día usé mi ordenador para buscar información y luego también jugué a videojuegos en la PlayStation con mis amigos por la noche. En el colegio, en la clase de informática, aprendí a utilizar un programa llamado procesador de textos. Me gustan los ordenadores porque son interesantes y pienso que también son muy prácticos en la vida cotidiana. Creo que también son importantes para encontrar un trabajo en el futuro porque estamos usando cada vez más las nuevas tecnologías en el mundo laboral y, en mi opinión, los ordenadores son las herramientas del futuro.

Después del colegio, hice mis deberes en línea con mis amigos. Me resulta más fácil trabajar en grupo para determinados temas. Después de terminar mis deberes, escuché canciones de mi cantante favorito en Spotify, saqué unas fotos con mi móvil y luego subí esas fotos a mi cuenta de Facebook. Sé que paso demasiado tiempo frente a una pantalla todos los días. Mis padres me dicen a menudo *[often]* que debería salir más de mi casa y hacer deporte al aire libre en lugar de perder el tiempo jugando en mi consola de videojuegos durante horas.

Por la noche hice una videollamada con mi novio y vi una serie en Netflix hasta las diez y media. Luego me cepillé los dientes y me acosté porque tenía que levantarme temprano a la mañana siguiente para ir a la escuela.

9. Answer the question on María's text

a. What did she eat and drink for breakfast?

b. What did she do while eating?

c. What did she do at 7:45?

d. What did she use the computer for? (2 details)

e. What type of software did she learn how to use in her IT lessons at school?

f. What are the tools of the future?

g. Who did she do her homework with?

h. What did she do with the photos she took?

10. Rearrange the information below in the same order as it occurs in the text

	I posted photos online
	Computers are the tool of the future
	I chatted online with my best friend
	I should get out more
	I like to take my time
	I listened to songs
	I brushed my teeth
	I did my homework

11. Translate into English

a. Móvil

b. En línea

c. Deberes

d. Pantalla

e. Canciones

f. Ordenadores

g. Informática

h. Cuenta

12. Complete

a. El viernes por la mañana me _____ a las seis y media con la alarma de mi móvil.

b. _____ un zumo de manzana y _____ una tostada con tomate.

c. _____ de casa a las ocho menos cuarto.

d. _____ mi ordenador para buscar información.

e. También _____ a videojuegos en línea.

f. Después de _____ mis deberes, _____ música en Spotify.

g. _____ fotos con mi teléfono. Luego _____ esas fotos en Facebook.

h. Por la tarde _____ los mensajes de Facebook y _____ una serie en Netflix.

contesté	hice	escuchaba	bebí	jugué	hacer
subí	desperté	desayuné	usé	salí	vi

13. Translate into Spanish

a. *I did my schoolwork*   H____ m__ d_____

b. *I made a videacall*   H_____ u__ v_____

c. *I listened to some songs*   E_____ c_____

d. *I brushed my teeth*   M_c_____ l__ d_____

e. *I used my computer*   U__ m__ o_____

f. *I played video games*   J____ a l__ v_____

g. *I finished my homework*   T_____ l_ d_____

h. *I drank an apple juice*   B____ u_ z___ d_ m_____

14. Complete with the missing letters

a. Alar_ _   *Alarm*

b. En lí_ _ _   *Online*

c. N_ _ _ _ _ _ _   *News*

d. H_ _ _ _   *I talked*

e. Table_   *Tablet*

f. Ordena_ _ _   *Computer*

g. Pan_ _ _ _ _   *Screen*

15. Translate into Spanish

a. Yesterday, I woke up with the alarm of my mobile phone

b. In the evening, I read some news online while listening to my favourite songs

c. Friday morning, I had breakfast while replying to my messages on WhatsApp

d. In the afternoon, we played video games online with our friends

e. On Saturday, I used my computer to look for information for my homework

f. Yesterday evening, I made a videacall with my cousins who live in Colombia

g. After finishing my homework, I watched a film on Netflix on my tablet

THE LANGUAGE GYM

Key questions

¿Para qué usaste la tecnología recientemente?	*What did you use technology for recently?*
¿Qué hiciste en tu ordenador la semana pasada?	*What did you do on your computer last week?*
¿Para qué utilizaste internet la semana pasada?	*What did you use the internet for last week?*
¿Qué hiciste con tu móvil para entretenerte ayer?	*What did you do on your mobile phone to entertain yourself yesterday?*
¿Cuándo tuviste tu primer móvil?	*When did you get your first mobile phone?*
¿Cuánto tiempo pasaste en internet ayer por la tarde/noche?	*How much time did you spend on the internet yesterday evening?*
¿Hiciste los deberes con la ayuda de internet la semana pasada? ¿Por qué ?	*Did you use the internet to help you with your homework last week? Why?*

Unit 2. Social media (present tense)

A la hora de comer	*At lunchtime*		**comentar en los foros** *to comment on forums*
A veces	*Sometimes*	**me encanta** *I love*	**conectarme a TikTok** *to connect (myself) to TikTok*
Cada dos días	*Every other day*	**me gusta** *I like*	**mirar las redes sociales** *to look at social media*
Cada noche	*Every evening/night*		**compartir vídeos graciosos** *to share funny videos*
Cuando puedo	*When I can*	**me gusta bastante** *I quite like*	**pasar tiempo en Facebook** *to spend time on Facebook*
Cuando tengo tiempo	*When I have time*	**me gusta mucho** *I like a lot*	**subir fotos a Instagram** *to post photos on Instagram*
En mi tiempo libre	*In my free time*		
Una vez al día	*Once a day*		

Gracias a las redes sociales, *Thanks to social media,*	
consigo *I manage to* **puedo** *I can*	**descubrir cosas nuevas** *discover new things* **distraerme de la vida real** *distract myself from real life* **hacer nuevos amigos** *make new friends* **mantenerme en contacto con mi familia que vive lejos** *stay in touch with my family who live far away* **ponerme al día con lo que está pasando en el mundo** *stay up to date with what is happening in the world*

Debido a las redes sociales, *Because of social media,*			
mucha gente *a lot of people*	**acaba** *end up*	**perdiendo la autoestima** *losing their self-esteem* **sintiéndose deprimida** *feeling depressed* **sintiéndose sola** *feeling alone*	
algunos jóvenes *some young people*	**se vuelven adictos** *become addicted*	**a internet** *to the internet* **a sus móviles** *to their phones*	
	desarrollan un trastorno del sueño *develop a sleep disorder* **pierden habilidades sociales** *lose social abilities*		

	recibo notificaciones *I receive notifications*		**a menudo** *often*
En las redes sociales, *On social media,*	**sigo a mi *influencer* favorito/a de …** *I follow my favourite ... influencer*	**moda / salud** *health / fashion*	**todos los días** *every day* **raramente** *rarely* **regularmente** *regularly*
	subo fotos a Instagram *I upload photos to Instagram*		
	le doy un 'me gusta' *I give a like*	**a las fotos de mis amigos/as** **a los TikToks de mis compañeros** **a mis YouTubers favoritos**	

1. Match

A la hora de comer	When I can
Cuando tengo tiempo	In the evening
En mi tiempo libre	Sometimes
Cuando puedo	Every other day
A veces	Once a day
Cada dos días	When I have time
Cada noche	In my free time
Una vez al día	At lunchtime
Por la noche	Every evening

2. Gapped translation

a._____ en los foros
To comment on forums

b._____ las redes sociales
To look at social media

c. Me gusta _____ a TikTok
I like to connect (myself) to TikTok

d. _____ tiempo en Facebook
To spend time on Facebook

e. _____ fotos a Instagram
To post photos on Instagram

f. _____ vídeos graciosos
To share funny videos

3. Positive or Negative?

Gracias a las redes sociales puedo…

a. …sentirme deprimido

b. …hacer nuevos amigos

c. …perder la autoestima

d. …volverme adicto

e. …descubrir cosas nuevas

f. …entretenerme

g. …ponerme al día con lo que está pasando en el mundo

h. …distraerme de la vida real

i. …perder habilidades sociales

4. Faulty translation: correct the English

a. Volverse adicto — *To become depressed*

b. Distraerse — *To get tired*

c. Hacer nuevos amigos — *To lose old friends*

d. Pasar tiempo — *To waste time*

e. Sentirse solo/a — *To feel depressed*

f. Perder la autoestima
To gain self-esteem

g. Desarrollar un trastorno del sueño
To develop an eating disorder

h. Mantenerse en contacto con la familia
To lose touch with one's family

5. Sentence puzzle

a. foros Me comentar en encanta los — *I love to comment on forums*

b. notificaciones Cada recibo día — *I receive notifications each day*

c. Mucha puede gente adicta volverse — *A lot of people can become addicted*

d. Sigo *influencer* mi a favorito — *I follow my favourite influencer*

e. deprimidos sentirse Algunos pueden jóvenes — *Some youngs people can feel depressed*

f. contacto Puedo mis mantenerme en parientes con — *I can stay in touch with my relatives*

g. Instagram Me conectarme a gusta — *I like to connect to Instagram*

h. a vídeos Tok Tik Subo — *I post videos on TikTok*

THE LANGUAGE GYM

18

6. Translate into English

a. Subo vídeos

b. Puedo mantenerme en contacto

c. Me encanta comentar

d. Recibo notificaciones

e. Descubro cosas nuevas

f. Puedo hacer nuevos amigos

g. Logro distraerme de la vida real

h. Sigo a mi *influencer* favorito

i. Pueden perder la autoestima

7. Broken sentences

Mucha gente	de la vida real
A menudo doy	de Instagram
Logro distraerme	puede deprimirse
Me encanta compartir	cosas nuevas
Algunos jóvenes desarrollan	al día
Recibo notificaciones	vídeos graciosos
Logro descubrir	un 'me gusta' en Facebook
Puedo ponerme	un trastorno del sueño

8. Gapped translation

a. *Every two days* _ _ _ _ dos días

b. *I post some videos* _ _ _ _ algunos vídeos

c. *I give a like* Le _ _ _ un 'me gusta'

d. *They can become addicted* Pueden volverse _ _ _ _ _ _ _

e. *Their self-esteem* Su _ _ _ _ _ _ _ _ _ _

f. *I love to comment* Me _ _ _ _ _ _ _ comentar

g. *Many people* Mucha _ _ _ _ _

9. Anagrams

a. *People* Geent

b. *To post* Sriub

c. *Regularly* Retemegunarl

d. *Relatives* Paserient

e. *New (masc. plural)* Nusove

f. *Depressed (fem. plural)* Diipremads

g. *To become* reseVovl

h. *Thanks to* Graasci a

10. Complete with the correct verb

a. Descubro _____ nuevas

b. Muchos jóvenes pueden_____ deprimidos

c. Me mantengo en _____ con mis amigos

d. Logro _____ de la vida real

e. Algunas personas _____ notificaciones a menudo

f. En mi tiempo libre me gusta _____ las redes sociales

g. Sigo a mi _____ de salud favorito todos los días

h. Cuando puedo _____ tiempo en Facebook

i. ____ un 'me gusta' a mis YouTubers favoritos

doy	contacto	*influencer*
cosas	paso	distraerme
mirar	acabar	reciben

11. Translate into Spanish

a. *To comment* C _ _ _ _ _ _ _

b. *To lose* P _ _ _ _ _

c. *To develop* D _ _ _ _ _ _ _ _ _

d. *To become* V _ _ _ _ _ _

e. *To discover* D _ _ _ _ _ _ _ _

f. *To feel* S _ _ _ _ _ s _

g. *To post* S _ _ _ _

h. *To share* C _ _ _ _ _ _ _ _

i. *To look* M _ _ _ _

j. *To follow* S _ _ _ _ _

k. *To find* E _ _ _ _ _ _ _ _

l. *To connect* C _ _ _ _ _ _ _ s _

12. Guided translation

a. *Thanks to social media*   G_____ a l____ r_____ s_____

b. *When I can*   C_____ p_____

c. *In my free time*   E_____ m____ t_____ l_____

d. *Every other day*   C_____ d____ d_____

e. *I stay in touch with*   M__ m_____ e__ c_____ c__

f. *I like to spend my time on*   M_ g_____ p_____ m_ t_____ e_

g. *To lose social abilities*   P_____ h_____ s_____

h. *New friends*   N_____ a_____

i. *Real life*   L_ v____ r_____

j. *Once a day*   U___ v_____ a_ d___

13. Complete with an appropriate word/phrase

a. Gracias a las redes sociales puedo mantenerme en contacto con _____

b. Debido a las redes sociales los jóvenes pueden _____ deprimidos

c. Todos los días paso mucho tiempo en _____

d. Cuando tengo tiempo _____ vídeos a TikTok

e. Me encanta dar 'me gusta' y comentar en _____

f. Logro distraerme de _____

g. Gracias a Instagram puedo _____

h. Gracias a internet puedo ponerme _____

14. Translate into Spanish

a. Thanks to Facebook, I can make new friends

b. Thanks to social media, I can discover new things

c. I can stay in touch with my family who lives far away

d. A lot of youngsters end up losing their self-esteem

e. I love to share photos and videos on Facebook

f. In my free time, I like to share funny videos

g. I love to comment on Facebook

h. I manage to distract myself

i. I can inform myself on what is happening in the world

TEXT 1 – Raúl (14 años, Valencia)

(1) Por lo general, a mediodía, me gusta conectarme a las redes sociales cuando tengo tiempo. Me encanta comentar en los foros y me gusta pasar tiempo en Facebook o Instagram para ver qué hacen mis amigos. Gracias a las redes sociales, puedo hacer nuevos amigos y distrarme de la vida real. Además, puedo ponerme al día con lo que está pasando en el mundo o buscar información. Paso más o menos media hora al día en internet.

(2) Desafortunadamente, debido a las redes sociales, en la actualidad, un gran número de jóvenes pasan muchísimo tiempo en las redes sociales. Algunos de ellos *[some of them]* acaban completamente adictos a sus móviles. Algunas personas pasan la mayor parte de su día en línea. Por lo tanto, *[therefore]* pierden las habilidades sociales ya que están constantemente delante de una pantalla y por eso pueden acabar sintiéndose solos.

(3) Debido a la pandemia del coronavirus, en este momento, los estudiantes a menudo se quedan solos *[left on their own]* en sus casas y pasan más tiempo en línea que antes. Muchos de ellos desarrollan un trastorno del sueño y algunos acaban sintiéndose deprimidos.

(4) No obstante, *[nonetheless]* las redes sociales también tienen cosas buenas. Gracias a internet podemos descubrir cosas nuevas y buscar información rápidamente. Yo logro mantenerme en contacto con mis amigos y familia que viven lejos de mí. Además, me gusta ponerme al día con lo que está pasando en el mundo. Aunque *[although]* internet tiene aspectos negativos, me encanta conectarme a Twitter, compartir vídeos graciosos con mi hermano mayor o subir fotos a Instagram. Lo hago todos los días porque me distrae de la vida real y me divierte.

15. Find the Spanish equivalent in paragraph 1

a. Social media

b. When I have the time

c. I spend time

d. What my friends do

e. To make new friends

f. Distract myself from

g. What is happening in the world

h. Half an hour a day

16. List the four negative consequences of the use of social networks mentioned in paragraph 2

a.

b.

c.

d.

17. Complete the translation of paragraph 3

_____ the coronavirus pandemic, _____ the

_____ students are _____ at

home and spend more time _____ than before.

Many of them _____ a sleep disorder and some

end up _____ depressed.

18. Find in paragraph 4 the following words and translate them into English

a. An adjective beginning with 'n'

b. A verb beginning with 'c'

c. A noun beginning with 'v'

d. An adjective beginning with 'r'

e. A pronoun beginning with 'l'

f. A verb beginning with 's'

TEXT 2 – Carmen (16 años, Gijón)

(1) Cuando tengo tiempo, me encanta pasar tiempo en Facebook y también me gusta subir fotos a Instagram todos lo días. Las redes sociales son muy importantes para mí porque puedo mantenerme en contacto con mis amigos. A menudo me conecto a Instagram porque recibo muchas notificaciones y puedo comentar los comentarios de los demás. No me gusta TikTok porque los vídeos que suben algunos jóvenes son aburridos.

(2) Gracias a las redes sociales puedo hacer nuevos amigos y hacer videollamadas con ellos. Mi mejor amiga tiene los mismos gustos que yo y sigue a los mismos *influencers* en Instagram, así que nos llevamos muy bien. Además, las redes sociales son una buena forma de distraerme de la vida real. También me encanta comprar en línea y, gracias a la inteligencia artificial (y los algoritmos), recibo publicidad *[advertisements]* de los productos que me gustan.

(3) Desafortunadamente, algunos de mis amigos acaban completamente adictos a las redes sociales. Mi amiga Noelia, por ejemplo, pasa la mayor parte de su tiempo en Facebook y no quiere salir conmigo, porque prefiere quedarse en casa con su móvil en lugar de salir al cine. Mateo, un chico de mi clase, desde la pandemia del coronavirus se siente deprimido y no le gusta hacer nada más que ver los vídeos en TikTok. Pasa demasiado tiempo en línea y por eso casi no sale de casa. Igual que Noelia.

(4) Creo que las redes sociales tienen ventajas e inconvenientes y todo depende de cómo las usemos. A mí me encanta conectarme a internet con mi tablet porque sin internet mi vida sería triste y aburrida. Por otro lado me gusta mucho salir con mis amigos a tomar un chocolate caliente o helados en una cafetería.

19. Complete based on paragraphs 1 and 2

a. When I have time, I love to _____ on Facebook.

b. Social media is very important to me because I can _____ with my friends.

c. _____ TikTok because the videos that some young people upload are boring.

d. Thanks to _____ _____ I can make new friends and make video calls with them.

e. My best friend _____ the same influencers on Instagram.

f. I also like to _____ photos to Instagram every day.

g. I also love shopping online, and _____ to artificial intelligence (and algorithms)…

h. I receive advertisements for the _____ I like.

i. So we _____ with each other very well.

20. Find the Spanish equivalent for the following English words/phrases in paragraphs 3 and 4

a. Unfortunately

b. Addicted

c. Most of her time

d. Go out with me

e. To stay at home

f. To spend time

g. Instead of going to the cinema

h. He spends

i. Almost doesn't leave home

j. Just like

k. Depends on

l. On the other hand

21. Choose the correct option from the three in bold

Desafortunadamente, hoy en día muchos jóvenes pasan **malo/demasiado/poco** tiempo en las redes sociales. Algunos de ellos pueden **envolverse/volarse/volverse** adictos a sus móviles. Debido a internet hay personas que desarrollan un trastorno del sueño y hasta pierden **les/las/los** habilidades sociales. Estas personas están constantemente **delante/en/dentro** de la pantalla y a menudo pueden acabar **sintiéndome/sintiéndose/sentirse** solas. Por otro **momento/sitio/lado**, gracias a internet, **volvemos/podemos/mantenemos** ponernos al día con lo que está pasando en el mundo y mantenernos en contacto con familia y amigos que viven lejos. También logramos distraernos de la vida **real/aburrida/loca** usando Facebook, TikTok e Instagram.

22. Translate into English

a. En general, a la hora de comer, me gusta conectarme a las redes sociales.

b. Mi amiga Verónica Palacín, por ejemplo, pasa la mayor parte de su tiempo en Facebook.

c. Tiene los mismos gustos que yo y sigue a los mismos *influencers*.

d. Las redes sociales son muy importantes para mí.

e. Creo que las redes sociales tienen ventajas e inconvenientes.

f. A mí me encanta conectarme a internet con mi tablet.

g. Sin internet mi vida sería triste y aburrida.

h. Todo depende de cómo lo usemos

23. Complete the missing words from the options below

Desafortunadamente, algunos de mis amigos _____ completamente _____ a las redes sociales. Mi amiga Noelia, por _____, pasa la mayor parte del tiempo en Facebook y no quiere _____ conmigo, porque prefiere quedarse en casa con su móvil en lugar de salir al cine. Mateo, un chico de mi clase, desde la pandemia del coronavirus se _____ deprimido y no le _____ hacer nada más que ver los vídeos en TikTok. Pasa _____ tiempo en línea y por eso casi no sale de casa. Igual _____ Noelia.

adictos	salir	demasiado	siente	gusta	acaban	que	ejemplo

24. Gapped translation: complete the translation of the Spanish text

Gracias a las redes sociales puedo hacer nuevos amigos y hacer videollamadas con ellos. Mi mejor amiga tiene los mismos gustos que yo y sigue a los mismos *influencers* en Instagram, así que nos llevamos muy bien. Además, las redes sociales son una buena forma de distraerme de la vida real. También me encanta comprar en línea y, gracias a la inteligencia artificial, recibo publicidad de los productos que me gustan.	*Thanks to social _____ I can make new friends and make video calls with _____. My best friend has the same _____ as me and she _____ the same influencers on Instagram, so we _____ with each other very well. Moreover, social media is a good way to _____ myself from real life. I _____ love shopping online, and thanks to artificial intelligence, I receive _____ for the products I like.*

25. Choose the correct translation

a. *Addicted* Adorables / Adictos / Adicción
b. *Time* Tempo / Tiempo / Timbo
c. *To share* Compartir / Partir / Compadre
d. *Fun* Diversión / Entrar / Divertido
e. *To become* Encontrar / Volverse / Pasar
f. *I receive* Recibo / Paso / Encuentro
g. *I look for* Busco / Recibo / Veo

h. *Good* Bueno / Malo / Adicto
i. *Online* De hecho / En línea / Internet
j. *World* Malo / Mundo / Consejo
k. *Lonely* Triste / Malo / Solo
l. *I spend time* Paso tiempo / No gasto / Es tiempo
m. *Relatives* Amigos / Parientes / Relativos
n. *Tastes* Gustos / Gastos / Juegos

26. Guided translation

a. *Many youngsters become addicted* M_____ j_____ s__ v_____ a_____
b. *I follow my favourite influencer* S____ a m__ i_____ f_____
c. *I spend a lot of time on social media* P____ m____ t_____ e__ l__ r_____ s_____
d. *They have pros and cons* T_____ v_____ e i_____
e. *They develop a sleeping disorder* D_____ u__ t_____ d___ s_____
f. *I like to comment on forums* M__ g_____ c_____ e__ l__ f_____
g. *Youngsters can lose their self-esteem* L__ j_____ p_____ p_____ l__ a_____

27. Translate into Spanish

a. Pros

b. Cons

c. Unfortunately

d. I can make new friends

e. I can discover new things

f. I use social media a lot

g. Many youngsters can become addicted

h. I post videos on Instagram

i. Carmen spends too much time on social media

j. Youngsters can feel depressed

k. I can stay in touch with my relatives

l. Because of social media, some people can end up feeling alone

28. Write a short text about the effects of social media. Say the following things

- Social media has pros and cons.
- Thanks to social media I can keep in touch with my relatives from Australia; I can make new friends; I can keep informed on what happens around the world and I also make new discoveries.
- Unfortunately, because of social media, some youngsters can develop obsessive behaviours, can become addicted; can feel depressed and lonely because they spend too much time in front of a screen.
- I use social media a lot and I follow some influencers; I post videos on Instagram; I comment on forums and make new friends.
- Unfortunately, my best friend Marc spends too much time on his phone and has become addicted. For that reason, he no longer goes out with his friends.

Key questions

¿Cómo usas las redes sociales normalmente?	*How do you usually use social media?*
Desde tu punto de vista, ¿cuáles son las ventajas de las redes sociales?	*According to you, what are the advantages of social media?*
En tu opinión, ¿cuáles son las desventajas de las redes sociales?	*In your opinion, what are the disadvantages of social media?*
¿Qué redes sociales te gustan? ¿Por qué?	*Which social media do you like? Why?*
¿Qué redes sociales no te gustan y por qué?	*Which social media don't you like and for what reasons?*
¿Cuándo, en general, te conectas a las redes sociales?	*When do you generally connect to social?*
¿Cuánto tiempo pasas en las redes sociales cada día?	*How much time do you spend on social media every day?*
¿Estás influenciado/a por las redes sociales? ¿Cómo?	*Are you influenced by social media? How?*
¿Quién son tus *influencers* favoritos?¿Por qué los sigues?	*Who are your favourite influencers? Why do you follow them?*
¿Conoces a alguien que se ha vuelto adicto/a a las redes sociales? Si es el caso, ¿qué tipo de comportamiento obsesivo han desarrollado?	*Do you know anyone who has become addicted to social media? If yes, what obsessive behaviours have they developed?*

Unit 2. Social media (past tense)

Anteayer	*The day before yesterday*	**compartí unas fotos** *I shared some photos*	**en Facebook** *on Facebook*
Ayer por la mañana	*Yesterday morning*	**escribí comentarios** *I wrote comments*	**en Instagram** *on Instagram*
Ayer por la tarde	*Yesterday afternoon*	**pasé tiempo** *I spent time*	**en las redes sociales** *on social media*
Ayer por la noche	*Yesterday evening*	**subí vídeos** *I posted videos*	**en Twitter** *on Twitter*
Hace una semana	*A week ago*	**me metí** *I *went*	**en Google** *on Google*
Hace unos días	*A few days ago*		
La semana pasada	*Last week*		

El fin de semana pasado, *Last weekend,*	**gracias a las redes sociales,** *thanks to social media,*	**conseguí / logré** *I managed to*	**descubrir cosas nuevas** *discover new things*
			hacer nuevos amigos *make new friends*
		pude *I was able to*	**evadirme de la realidad** *distract myself from real life*
			informarme sobre lo que pasa en el mundo *inform myself about what is happening in the world*

Desde el nacimiento de las redes sociales *Since the birth of social media*	**algunos adolescentes** *some teenagers*	**han** *have*	**desarrollado un comportamiento obsesivo** *developed an obsessive behaviour*
Durante la pandemia *During the pandemic*	**muchas personas** *a lot of people*		**echado en falta las relaciones cara a cara** *missed having face to face interactions*
En los últimos años, debido a las redes sociales *In recent years, because of social media*	**muchos jóvenes** *many youngsters*	**se han** *have*	**sentido aislados** *felt isolated*
			vuelto adictos *become addicted*

Ayer, antes de acostarme, *Yesterday, before going to bed,*	**leí un artículo sobre...** *I read an article about...*		
	recibí notificaciones *I received notifications*		
	le di un 'me gusta' a *I gave a like to a*	**la foto de mi amigo** *my friend's photo*	
		un vídeo que me gustó *a video that I liked*	
	subí una foto a mi Instagram *I uploaded a photo to my Instagram*		
	vi un vídeo en YouTube *I watched a video on YouTube*		
	seguí a *I followed*	**un nuevo *influencer* de** *a new ... influencer*	**moda/salud** *fashion/health*

Author's note: "*Me metí en internet*" literally means I went inside the internet.

1. Match

Ayer por la mañana	I had
Escribí comentarios	In recent years
Hace unos días	I managed to
Recibí	Many teenagers
Aislados	I followed
Tuve	Some people
En los últimos años	A few days ago
Muchos adolescentes	Isolated
Seguí	I received
La vida real	In the world
Alguna gente	I was able to
Pude	Yesterday morning
En el mundo	Real life
Logré	I wrote comments

2. Complete the words then translate into English

a. Escribí com_ _ _ _ _ _ _ _

b. Pasé t_ _ _ _ _

c. Ayer por la t_ _ _ _

d. Muchos ado_ _ _ _ _ _ _ _

e. Ante_ _ _ _

f. Mu_ _ _ ge_ _ _

g. Con_ _ _ _í hacer nuevos amigos

h. Un compor_ _ _ _ _ _ _ _

i. Seguid _ _

j. Las re_ _ _ soci _ _ _ _

k. Pu_ _ ha _ _ r

3. Phrase puzzle

a. semana Hace una	A week ago
b. nuevos amigos Hice	I made new friends
c. últimos En años los	In recent years
d. vuelto Se adictos han	They have become addicted
e. *influencers* a nuevos Seguí	I followed new influencers
f. informarme Pude sobre	I was able to inform myself on
g. las Gracias a sociales redes	Thanks to social media
h. fotos unas Compartí con	I shared some photos with
i. aislados han Se sentido	They have felt isolated
j. Leí un artículo interesante	I read an interesting article

4. Anagrams: unjumble and translate the following words/phrases

a. ropCatomomtien oobsseiv

b. Dirrescbu sacos nuaves

c. cHea uan samane

d. Síub sveído

e. Mousch asscentdolee

f. En cuneta im ed Gogloe

g. Pued chare asgimo

h. Nuoves rinsfulence

i. Diodeb a sla reeds liasesoc

5. Translate into English

a. Ayer por la tarde recibí muchas notificaciones en Instagram

b. Debido a las redes sociales muchos jóvenes se han vuelto adictos

c. Anteayer pude hacer nuevos amigos

d. Por la tarde pasé tiempo en Facebook y subí unas fotos bonitas

e. La semana pasada descubrí cosas nuevas

f. Gracias a las redes sociales, seguí a un nuevo *influencer* de salud

g. Hace unos días me metí en Instagram y escribí unos comentarios

h. Ayer por la noche le di un 'me gusta' a la foto de mi amiga

i. Pude distraerme de la realidad

6. Complete

a. En ___ mundo

b. Le __ un 'me gusta'

c. _____ notificaciones

d. Ayer___ ___ mañana

e. Evadirme ___ la realidad

f. En ___ redes _____

g. __ fin de _____ pasado

h. _____ comentarios

i. Antes __ acostarme

j. _____ cinco minutos

7. Gapped translation

a. Ayer _____ __ _____ , me _____ en Instagram *Yesterday evening, I went on Instagram*

b. La semana pasada, _____ hacer _____ amigos *Last week I managed to make new friends*

c. _____ notificaciones _____ cinco _____ *I received notifications every five minutes*

d. _____ a un _____ influencer de _____ *I followed a new health influencer*

e. Le __ un 'me _____' a la _____de mi novia *I gave a like to my girlfriend's photo*

f. Pude _____ sobre lo ___ pasa *I was able to inform myself on what is happening*

g. _____ tiempo en ___ redes _____ *I spent time on social media*

8. Sentence puzzle

a. por Ayer Facebook la tarde me conecté a una hora. genial! durante ¡Estuvo
Yesterday afternoon, I connected (myself) to Facebook for one hour. It was great!

b. El gracias fin las de sociales semana descubrir pasado, a redes conseguí nuevas cosas
Last weekend, thanks to social media, I managed to discover new things

c. Desde algunos el nacimiento han de las desarrollado redes obsesivo sociales, adolescentes comportamiento un
Since the birth of social media, some teenagers have developed an obsessive behaviour

d. En los redes últimos debido años, a jóvenes las sociales, muchos han relaciones echado en falta cara a cara
In recent years, because of social media, many youngsters have lacked face to face relations

e. Hace días unos recibí notificaciones minutos cada cinco
A few day ago I received notifications every five minutes

f. La semana seguidores pasada subí unos tuve vídeos en TikTok y nuevos
Last week I posted some videos on TikTok and I had new followers

9. Tangled translation: into Spanish

a. Ayer **morning**, **I spent** tiempo en las **social media**

b. Conseguí **make** nuevos **friends** en Facebook

c. Conseguí **distract myself** de la **real life**

d. **During** la tarde, seguí a **new influencers**

e. Recibí nuevas **notifications every** cinco **minutes**

f. Muchos **young people** se han vuelto **addicted**

g. **I have** amigos que se han **felt** aislados

h. Hace **some** días **I shared** unas fotos **on** Instagram

i. Pude **inform myself** sobre lo que **happening** en **the** mundo

10. Translate into Spanish

a. Behaviour	j. I had
b. Many	k. To discover
c. During	l. Real life
d. I followed	m. Teenagers
e. Loneliness	n. A lot of people
f. New things	o. Addicted
g. New friends	p. I managed to
h. A feeling	q. I was able to
i. I went	r. I received

Conversación entre amigos (1) (Part 1)

María: Cuéntame, ¿qué hiciste en las redes sociales la semana pasada? *[Tell me, what did you do on social media last week?]*

Carlos: La semana pasada me metí en las redes sociales porque estaba de vacaciones en Andalucía, así que tenía tiempo. Comenté en Facebook y también me metí en Instagram para ver qué estaban haciendo mis amigos.

María: En tu opinión, ¿cuáles son las ventajas e inconvenientes de las redes sociales? *[According to you, what are the pros and cons of social media?]*

Carlos: Ante todo *[first of all]*, la comunicación. Recientemente, gracias a las redes sociales, logré hacer nuevos amigos y así conocí a mi novia. Segundo, entretenimiento. Yo creo que las redes sociales son una buena manera *[a good way]* de distraerse de la vida real y de estar informado en tiempo real de lo que pasa en el mundo.

María: ¿Cuánto tiempo pasaste en las redes sociales ayer, por ejemplo? *[How much time did you spend on social media yesterday, for example?]*

Carlos: Ayer pasé una hora entera en las redes sociales, lo cual es bastante razonable en mi opinión. Me metí en Facebook y comenté en algunos foros y luego compartí fotos de mis vacaciones en Andalucía en Instagram. También subí tres vídeos divertidos. Fue relajante y entretenido.

11. Find the Spanish for the following

a. *Last week*   L_ s_____ p_____

b. *I was on holidays*   E_____ de v_____

c. *I had time*   T_____ t_____

d. *What my friends were doing*
Q_ e_____ h_____ m_ a_____

e. *Tell me (about)*   C_____

f. *According to you*   E_ t_ o_____

g. *The advantages*   L__ v_____

h. *Recently*   R_____

i. *I met*   C_____

j. *My girlfriend*   M_ n____

k. *I believe that*   C_____ q__

l. *A good way*   U_ b___ m_____

m. *Real life*   L_ v___ r_____

n. *In the world*   E_ e_ m_____

o *You did*   H_____

p. *Yesterday for example* A__ p__ e_____

q. *On a few forums*   E_ a_____ f_____

r. *In real time*   E__ t_____ r_____

s. *Entertaining*   E_____

12. Complete the translation of Carlos' last answer

Yesterday, I _____ one whole hour on social media, which is _____ reasonable in my _____ . I went on Facebook _____ I commented on ___ _____ forums and _____ I shared some _____ from my _____ in Andalusia on Instagram. I _____ posted three _____ videos, it _____ relaxing and _____ .

13. Complete the text below with the options provided in the table

_____, debido a las redes_____, muchos ___ mis _____ se han _____ completamente adictos a sus _____. Mi _____ Rubén _____ todo su _____ en _____. ¡Es un problema! ¡Ya ni siquiera _____ al fútbol!

desafortunadamente	amigo	pasa	vuelto
internet	amigos	de	tiempo
móviles	problema	juega	sociales

Conversación entre amigos (1) (Part 2)

María: En tu experiencia, ¿cuáles han sido los inconvenientes de las redes sociales? *[In your experience, what have been the disadvantages of social media?]*

Carlos: Desafortunadamente, debido a las redes sociales, muchos de mis amigos se han vuelto completamente adictos a sus teléfonos móviles. Mi amigo Cristobal pasa todo su tiempo en internet. ¡Es un problema! ¡Ya ni siquiera juega al fútbol ni hace surf en la playa!

María: En tu opinión, ¿qué ha cambiado desde el nacimiento de las redes sociales? *[In your opinion, what has changed since the birth of social media?]*

Carlos: En mi opinión, las redes sociales han cambiado la forma en que vivimos. Ayudaron en la comunicación y ahora es gratis e instantáneo. En estos días es muy fácil mantenerse en contacto con tus amigos, incluso si están en otro país.

14. True, False or Not mentioned?

a. Because of social media, a lot of Carlos' friends are addicted to their phones

b. His friend Cristobal spends all his time playing football and surfing

c. Social media is expensive for users

d. Social media has slowed down communication

e. Social media is designed to make people dependant on them

f. Carlos thinks social media has transformed the way we work

g. Nowadays it's complicated to stay in touch with your friends

h. You can't use social media to communicate from one country to another

15. Answer the following questions about part 1 and 2 of María and Carlos' conversation

a. Where was Carlos last week?

b. Why did he go on Facebook and Instagram last week? (2 details)

c. Recently, what has he been able to do thanks to social media? (2 details)

d. What are the two strong points he mentions in favour of social media?

e. What did he do on Instagram yesterday? (2 details)

f. How was it? (2 adjectives)

g. What has happened to a lot of his friends?

h. What does he say about his friend Cristobal? (2 details)

i. In his opinion, what has changed with social media? (2 details)

16. Split sentences: join the two chunks in each column to make logical sentences then translate them

1	2	English translation
Mis amigos se han vuelto	así que tenía tiempo	
Compartí algunas	mi nueva novia	
Ayudaron en	en las redes sociales	
Estaba de vacaciones	completamente adictos	
Me metí	fotos de mis vacaciones	
Es fácil mantenerse	la comunicación	
Conocí a	en contacto con amigos	

Conversación entre amigos (2) (Part 1)

Fernando: Cuéntame, ¿qué hiciste en las redes sociales el fin de semana pasado? *[Tell me, what did you do on social media last weekend?]*

Sara: El fin de semana pasado me metí en Facebook y subí fotos en Instagram. Las redes sociales son muy importantes para mí porque me permiten estar en contacto con mis amigos. El sábado recibí notificaciones durante todo el día, lo que debo admitir *[which I must admit]* que fue una gran distracción. El domingo me metí en Twitter, pero tengo que decir que me gusta menos esta red social, porque en mi opinión es un poco aburrida.

Fernando: En tu opinión, ¿cuáles son las ventajas de las redes sociales? *[In your opinion, what are the advantages of social media?]*

Sara: Gracias a las redes sociales puedo conocer a gente nueva y así conocí a mi mejor amiga Julia hace dos años. Inmediatamente nos llevamos bien, porque compartimos las mismas pasiones. De igual manera *[In the same way]*, logré conocer a mi novio en Instagram mirando los perfiles de los chicos de mi universidad. Entonces, para mí, el punto fuerte de las redes sociales es que ahora es muy fácil hacer nuevos amigos.

17. Find the Spanish for the following

a. For me

b. To stay in touch

c. They allow me

d. Sunday

e. I connected to

f. I must say

g. Less

h. A bit

i. In my opinion

j. The strength

k. Boring

l. I can meet new people

m. That's how I met

n. In the same way

o. I managed to meet

p. The profiles

q. To make new friends

18. Complete the translation from the first question and answer

Fernando: _____ me, what did you _____ on social media _____ weekend?

Sara: Last weekend, _____ on Facebook and I _____ some photos on Instagram. Social media is _____ important ____ ____ , because it allows me to _____ in touch _____ my friends. On _____ , I _____ notifications all _____ long, which I must _____ was a _____ distraction. On _____ , I connected to Twitter, _____ I _____ say that I like this social media _____ , because it is ___ _____ boring ___ ___ _____ .

19. Correct the spelling errors

a. De igaul manera

b. Una gran distraction

c. Logre conocer a

d. Le que debo admit

e. Nos levamos bien

f. Ester en contact

20. Anagrams

a. *Boring (fem)*   ibAurdra

b. *Boys*   icCosh

c. *The same way*   eD gialu ranmea

d. *I met*   noCcío

e. *My boyfriend*   iM oiovn

Conversación entre amigos (2) (Part 2)

Fernando: ¿Cómo usaste las redes sociales ayer, por ejemplo?

Sara: Anoche pude comprar en línea con el dinero que me dieron por mi cumpleaños hace dos semanas. Gracias a la inteligencia artificial (y a los algoritmos) recibí anuncios de productos en oferta *[on sale]* de las marcas que sigo en Instagram. Así que fue muy conveniente para ir de compras. Compré ropa bonita con una buena relación calidad-precio.

Fernando: ¿Cuándo fue la última vez que te metiste en Instagram? ¿Qué hiciste? *[When did you go on Instagram for the last time? What did you do?]*

Sara: La última vez que me metí en Instagram fue esta mañana. Publiqué dos fotos y respondí a los mensajes. Luego le di un 'me gusta' a las fotos y vídeos de mis *influencers* favoritos y por supuesto de mis amigos. Fue entretenido y también encontré algunos vídeos cortos *[reels]* muy divertidos.

21. True, False or Not mentioned?

a. According to Sara, artificial intelligence (and algorithms) has made shopping easier

b. Her birthday was yesterday

c. All the clothes she liked were sold out

d. She follows clothes brands on Instagram

e. She bought expensive, but cheap quality clothes

f. The last time she went on Instagram was yesterday morning

g. She posted two videos and answered her messages

h. Then she liked the photos of her favourite influencers

i. She didn't like any of her friends' posts

j. She found the reels very boring and she doesn't like them

22. Translate the following paragraphs into Spanish

Last weekend, on Saturday, I went on Instagram and I posted some photos and some videos of my holidays. It was relaxing and I only spent one hour in total on social media. Then, I answered my messages on WhatsApp and I commented on some forums. On Sunday, I did some shopping online and I bought some new clothes. I love my new trousers!

Recently, thanks to social media, I managed to make new friends and I have also met my girlfriend like this. I believe it is a good way to stay in touch with people. For my birthday, I was given *[me dieron]* a mobile phone, so lately *[últimamente]* I have been able to distract myself on Facebook. Yesterday evening, I also shared some photos on Instagram and I received notifications every five minutes. It was a big distraction!

23. Complete with an appropriate word

a. Mis amigos se han vuelto _____ a sus móviles

b. Ayer por la tarde, encontré unos vídeos muy _____

c. Tengo que _____ que _____ una gran distracción

d. _____ un 'me gusta' a las fotos y _____ los mensajes

e. En total _____ una hora en Instagram

f. _____ ropa bonita con una buena _____ calidad-precio

24. Write a 120-word composition including the following points

- What you did on social media last weekend and how it was

- In your experience, what are the strengths of social media

- What are the negative points

- How you used technology yesterday

Key questions

¿Cómo utilizaste las redes sociales ayer por la tarde?	*How did you use social media yesterday afternoon?*
Háblame sobre lo que hiciste en las redes sociales el fin de semana pasado	*Tell me about what you did on social media last weekend*
¿Qué te gustó hacer en las redes sociales ayer por la noche?	*What did you enjoy doing on social media yesterday evening?*
Según tú, ¿qué ha cambiado desde el nacimiento de las redes sociales?	*According to you, what has changed since the birth of social media?*
¿Cuáles han sido los aspectos negativos asociados con las redes sociales en los últimos años?	*What have been the negative points associated to social media in recent years?*
¿Cuándo fue la última vez que te metiste en Instagram? ¿Y qué hiciste?	*When did you last go on Instagram? And what did you do?*
¿Cuánto tiempo pasaste en las redes sociales el sábado pasado?	*How much time did you spend on social media last Saturday?*
¿Te han influenciado últimamente las redes sociales? ¿Cómo?	*Have you recently been influenced by social media? How?*

Unit 3. Mobile technology (present tense)

Actualmente, *Currently,* **En este momento,** *At this moment,* **Hoy en día,** *Nowadays,*	**en nuestra sociedad** *in our society,*	**la tecnología móvil** *mobile technology*	**es atractiva porque es multifuncional** *is attractive because it is multifunctional* **es fundamental en el mundo del trabajo** *is indispensable in the world of work* **es vital para nuestras tareas diarias** *is vital for our daily tasks*
			está omnipresente en nuestras vidas *is everywhere in our lives*

A menudo uso *I often use* **Me gusta utilizar** *I like to use* **Siempre uso** *I always use*	**mi altavoz portátil** *my portable speaker* **mi móvil** *my mobile phone* **mi portátil** *my laptop* **mi reloj inteligente** *my smartwatch* **mi tablet** *my tablet*	**porque es** *because it is*	**eficaz y compacto/a** *efficient and compact* **fácil viajar con él/ella** *easy to travel with it* **ligero/a** *light* **práctico/a** *practical* **rápido/a y entretenido/a** *fast and entertaining*

Una de las ventajas de la tecnología móvil es *One of the advantages of mobile technology is*	**el acceso a aplicaciones modernas** *access to modern apps* **la capacidad de comunicarse fuera de la oficina** *the ability to communicate outside of the office* **la capacidad de pagar de forma remota** *the ability to pay remotely* **que es una fuente de entretenimiento** *that it is a source of entertainment*

Una de las desventajas de la tecnología móvil es que *One of the disadvantages of mobile technology is*	**es demasiado fácil entrar en nuestras redes sociales** *it's too easy to check our social networks* **los productos nuevos son muy caros** *new products are very expensive* **nos distrae cuando recibimos notificaciones** *it distracts us when we receive notifications* **nos distrae de nuestros estudios** *it distracts us from our studies*

THE LANGUAGE GYM

1. Match

Actualmente	Tablet
Hoy en día	Light
De aquí en adelante	Nowadays
Ligero	A watch
Fácil	The price
El altavoz portátil	From now on
Tablet	Easy
Una fuente	Outside of
Un reloj	Portable speaker
Fuera de	Currently
El precio	A source

2. Complete with the missing letters

a. *A tablet*   Una table_

b. *Multifunctional*   Multif_ncion_ _

c. *Disadvantage*   Desven_ _ _a

d. *Technology*   Te_nolog_ _

e. *Capacity*   Capacid_ _

f. *Products*   Produ_ _ _ _

g. *To pay*   Pa _ _ _

h. *Everywhere*   Omnipr_sent_

i. *Source*   Fuen_ _

3. Sentence puzzle

a. porque La móvil multifuncional tecnología es es atractiva
Mobile technology is attractive because it is multifunctional

b. entretenimiento Una de las tecnología ventajas de fuente la móvil es que es una de
One of the advantages of mobile technology is that it is a source of entertainment

c. Me entretenido gusta porque utilizar mi y móvil es rápido
I like to use my mobile phone because it is fast and entertaining

d. causa Una de las distracción desventajas de tecnología la móvil es la que
One of the disadvantages of mobile technology is the distractions it causes

e. porque Siempre fácil con uso mi tablet es ella viajar
I always use my tablet because it is easy to travel with it

f. altavoz Me eficaz gusta utilizar mi portátil compacto porque es y
I like to use my portable speaker because it is effective and compact

4. Complete with the missing words choosing the correct options provided below

Las ventajas de la tecnología móvil

a. Es una fuente de _____   *It is a source of entertainment*

b. La capacidad de _____ ...   *The ability to communicate...*

c. ..._____ de la oficina   *...outside of the office*

d. Es _____   *It is multifunctional*

e. La _____ de pagar de forma remota   *The ability to pay remotely*

f. La flexibilidad _____   *Geographical flexibility*

g. El _____ a aplicaciones modernas   *Access to modern apps*

fuera	capacidad	geográfica	comunicarse	entretenimiento	multifuncional	acceso

5. Look for the Spanish translation in the wordsearch and add the accents when needed

t	s	j	a	g	b	w	f	e	c	a	p	a	c	i	d	a	d
d	e	f	i	c	a	z	j	n	o	a	l	ñ	u	t	z	q	g
r	n	t	f	o	v	b	m	t	d	l	y	j	k	a	i	j	n
l	s	ñ	á	r	u	b	n	r	s	t	h	p	m	r	w	c	z
i	r	n	c	t	i	o	d	e	x	a	a	e	o	e	h	r	m
g	d	g	i	z	q	v	t	t	u	v	p	r	c	a	l	k	b
e	k	y	l	w	b	m	q	e	b	o	a	e	f	s	u	y	j
r	u	t	i	l	i	z	o	n	e	z	a	c	c	e	s	o	l
o	y	w	n	a	a	v	b	i	a	t	r	a	c	t	i	v	o
c	s	t	m	o	ñ	j	t	d	g	e	i	m	q	n	b	w	p
o	l	r	p	y	b	r	x	o	d	p	r	á	c	t	i	c	o
l	o	m	n	i	p	r	e	s	e	n	t	e	t	y	s	z	t

a. Omnipresent

b. I use

c. Ability

d. Practical (*masc.*)

e. Attractive

f. Easy

g. Light (*fem.*)

h. Access

i. Effective

j. Tasks

k. Speaker

l. Entertaining

6. Gapped translation

a. Las tareas diarias   *Daily* _____

b. Es atractivo   *It is* _____

c. Mi altavoz portátil   *My portable* _____

d. Es fácil viajar con él   *It is* _____ *to travel with it*

e. Fuera de la oficina   *Outside* _____

f. Una fuente de entretenimiento   *A source of* _____

g. Son muy caros   *They are very* _____

h. Busco en mi tablet   *I* _____ *in my tablet*

i. La capacidad de comunicarse   *The* _____ *to communicate*

j. Una fuente de información   *A* _____ *of information*

k. Flexibilidad geográfica   *Geographical* _____

l. Mi reloj inteligente   *My* _____

m. Es eficaz y compacto   *It is* _____ *and compact*

7. Translate into English

a. La tecnología móvil

b. Es multifuncional

c. Las tareas diarias

d. Actualmente

e. De aquí en adelante

f. Es una fuente de entretenimiento

g. Es muy ligero/a

h. Pagar de forma remota

i. Una de las ventajas

j. En el mundo del trabajo

k. Fuera de la oficina

l. Un altavoz portátil

8. Break the flow

a. Unadelasdesventajasdelatecnologíamóvilesquelosproductosnuevossonmuycaros

b. Enestemomentolatecnologíamóvilestáomnipresenteennuestrasociedad

c. Siempreusomitabletporqueesmuyligeraeficazycompacta

d. Unadelasventajasdelatecnologíamóvileslaflexibilidadgeográfica

e. Megustautilizarmiportátilporqueesrápidoyentretenido

f. Actualmentelatecnologíaesfundamentalenelmundodeltrabajo

g. Latecnologíamóvilesprácticaperonosdistraecuandorecibimosnotificaciones

h. Enestemomentoesdemasiadofácilentrarennuestrasredessociales

i. Amenudousomirelojinteligenteporqueesprácticoperomedistraedemisestudios

9. Guided translation

a. *Mobile technology* L_ t_____ m_____

b. *One of the advantages* U__ d__ l__ v_____

c. *In the world of work* E_ e__ m_____ d_ t_____

d. *It's effective and compact* E__ e_____ y c_____

e. *It's multifunctional* E_ m_____

f. *Nowadays* H___ e_ d____

g. *Modern applications* L__ a_____ m_____

h. *New products are very expensive*
L__ p_____ n_____ s__ m___ c_____

10. Complete with the missing letters

a. En este mo_ _ _to

b. Es vi_ _ _

c. La tec_ _ _ogía m_ _ _l

d. H_ _ en d_ _

e. Mi re_ _ _ inteli_ _ _ _ _

f. Ef_ _ _ _ y comp_ _to

g. Es f_ _ _l via_ _ _ co_ el_ _

11. Translate into Spanish

a. Mobile technology is a source of entertainment

b. One of its (*sus*) advantages is the ability to pay remotely

c. It is easy to travel with my laptop because it is light

d. One of the disadvantages is that new products are very expensive

e. Another disadvantage is that it causes distractions

f. Mobile technology is very attractive because it is multifunctional

g. Nowadays, it is vital for our daily tasks

h. It is everywhere in our lives and indispensable in the world of work

i. I use my mobile phone and my smartwatch every day because they are practical and effective

TEXT 1 – Juan (21 años, Segovia)

(1) Actualmente, en nuestra sociedad, la tecnología móvil es indispensable tanto en el mundo laboral como en la casa. La tecnología móvil está omnipresente en nuestras vidas. Por ejemplo, todos los días, me gusta utilizar mi portátil para trabajar ya que es muy ligero y fácil de llevar. Además utilizo mi móvil porque es rápido y entretenido, así como práctico, para estar en contacto con mis amigos y mi familia.

(2) En este momento, la tecnología móvil es atractiva porque es multifuncional y, muy a menudo, los dispositivos electrónicos inventados en los últimos años tienen más de una función. Por ejemplo, uso mi tablet tanto para hacer búsquedas, como para jugar a videojuegos en línea o para ver películas en Netflix. Igualmente, uso mi móvil para enviar mensajes a mis amigos, para sacar fotos, para escuchar música y para leer las noticias cada mañana. Me encanta porque es práctico, eficaz y compacto.

(3) Una de las ventajas de la tecnología móvil es, sin ninguna duda, el acceso a las aplicaciones modernas donde quiera que vayamos, así como el hecho de siempre estar conectados a internet. Esto da la posibilidad de comunicarnos fuera de la oficina, lo que nos permite más flexibilidad geográfica. Hoy en día, muchas personas teletrabajan, es decir, trabajan desde casa algunos días de la semana. Este fenómeno se ha desarrollado notablemente durante la pandemia del coronavirus y gracias a la teconología móvil se ha hecho posible.

(4) Uno de los mayores inconvenientes de la tecnología móvil es el costo elevado de los productos. Aunque ahora son menos costosos que al principio, estos dispositivos modernos están lejos de ser asequibles y siguen siendo muy caros para el consumidor medio. Por otro lado, también son una gran fuente de distracción para todo el mundo y a veces generan comportamientos obsesivos en algunas personas.

12. Find in paragraph 1 the Spanish equivalent for the following

a. The world of work

b. Electronic devices

c. From now on

d. In our lives

e. I like using

f. It is light

g. I also use

h. Entertaining

i. Practical

13. Complete the translation of paragraph 2 below

_____, in our society, mobile technology is _____ , both in the wold of work and at _____. Mobile technology is omnipresent in our _____. For instance, every day I like to use my _____ to work seeing as it is very _____ and _____ to carry. Moreover, I use my mobile because it is _____ and entertaining, as well as _____, to stay _____ with my friends and family.

14. Answer the following questions on paragraphs 3 and 4

a. What is one of the advantages of mobile technology?

b. What is 'teletrabajar'?

c. What is a major disadvantage of mobile technology?

d. What are two other problems associated with mobile technology?

TEXT 2 – Pilar (13 años, Bilbao)

(1) Hoy en día, la teconología móvil es vital para nuestras tareas cotidianas. No hay un solo día que no utilice mi teléfono móvil, mi reloj inteligente o mi tablet. Siempre los necesito. Estos dispositivos inteligentes están ahora omnipresentes en mi rutina diaria. Por ejemplo, utilizo mi móvil para despertarme cada mañana. A continuación, miro las noticias en mi tablet mientras desayuno y leo los mensajes en mi reloj inteligente de camino al colegio.

(2) Me encanta usar mi teléfono móvil para escuchar música en Spotify. Es práctico, ya que lo puedo usar con mis auriculares con cancelación de ruido o con mis altavoces portátiles. La calidad del sonido ahora es increíble en comparación con el tamaño del altavoz ; es eficaz y compacto. También uso a menudo mi tablet ya que es ligera para viajar con ella. Raramente me separo de ella porque la necesito para hacer mi trabajo escolar y también en mi tiempo libre para divertirme y jugar a videojuegos o ver series en Netflix.

(3) En mi opinión, una de las ventajas de la tecnología móvil es la capacidad de pagar de forma remota. ¡Ya no es necesario llevar dinero en efectivo contigo! Ahora puedes pagar en línea y sin contacto a través de aplicaciones de pago móvil, lo que también es más rápido y fácil. Siempre lo uso para ir de compras y me resulta muy práctico porque no tengo que sacar dinero del cajero automático con mi tarjeta bancaria constantemente.

(4) En mi opinión, una de las desventajas de la tecnología móvil es el alto precio de estos dispositivos electrónicos. A pesar de que los precios en general están cayendo, el precio de un nuevo teléfono móvil u ordenador portátil sigue siendo muy alto. Además, la tecnología está cambiando tan rápido que al cabo de unos años estos dispositivos ya están obsoletos. La otra desventaja es que estos aparatos generan muchas distracciones para sus usuarios, lo que puede resultar en una pérdida de tiempo considerable si no tenemos cuidado.

15. Translate into English the following phrases taken from paragraph 1

a. Las tareas cotidianas

b. Un solo día

c. Siempre los necesito

d. Estos dispositivos inteligentes

e. Para despertarme cada mañana

f. Mientras desayuno

g. En mi reloj inteligente

16. Find the Spanish equivalent in paragraph 2

a. My noise-cancelling earphones

b. My portable speaker

c. Sound

d. Compared to

e. The size of the speaker

f. Light

g. I need it

h. In order to have fun

17. Complete the following sentences based on paragraphs 3 and 4

a. In my opinion, one of the advantages of mobile technology is the ability to _____

b. There is no longer the need to _____ _____!

c. Now one can pay online and contactless thanks to _____

d. One of the disadvantages is the _____ _____.

e. Even though the prices are decreasing, the cost of a new mobile phone and of a new laptop _____.

f. Moreover, technology evolves so fast that _____ _____.

18. Complete with the correct option choosing from the options below

La tecnología _____ ahora es indispensable en el _____ del trabajo así como en el hogar. Estos _____ electrónicos portátiles están omnipresentes en nuestras vidas. Por ejemplo, todos los días, me encanta usar mi _____ para mi trabajo porque es muy _____ y por lo tanto es muy fácil de viajar con ella. También siempre _____ desde mi móvil porque es rápido y _____, pero también conveniente para comunicarme con mis amigos y parientes. Me encanta _____ mi móvil para escuchar música en Spotify. Es conveniente, porque puedo usarlo con mis _____ con cancelación de ruido o con mi _____ portátil. También uso a menudo mi _____ porque lo necesito en la universidad para mis _____ diarias y también durante mi tiempo libre para _____ y jugar a videojuegos o ver series _____ Netflix.

auriculares	utilizar	móvil	portátil	tablet	tareas	trabajo
en	dispositivos	divertirme	eficaz	mundo	ligera	altavoz

19. Faulty translation: correct the English

a. Nuestras tareas diarias	*Our daily lives*
b. Estos dispositivos electrónicos	*These electronic games*
c. Utilizo mi portátil	*I like my laptop*
d. Raramente me separo de él	*I rarely take it with me*
e. Siempre los necesito	*I always use them*
f. Es rápido y eficaz	*It is fast and useful*
g. El alto precio	*The high level*
h. Un altavoz portáble	*A portable microphone*

20. Translate into English

a. Una de las desventajas de la tecnología móvil es el alto precio de los dispositivos electrónicos

b. Una de las ventajas de la tecnología móvil es la capacidad de pagar de forma remota

c. La tecnología móvil es vital para nuestras tareas diarias

d. Esos aparatos causan muchas distracciones para sus usuarios

e. A menudo uso mi tablet porque es ligera y además es multifuncional

f. Cada día uso mi móvil porque es rápido y divertido

g. Utilizo mi móvil para despertarme cada mañana

h. Una de las ventajas de la tecnología móvil es el acceso a las aplicaciones modernas vayas donde vayas

21. Guided translation

a. *Mobile technology is vital*   L_ t_____ m_____ e__ v_____

b. *I always use my mobile phone*   S_____ u____ m____ m_____

c. *One of the advantages is…*   U_ d_ l___ v_____ e__ …

d. *I often use my tablet because it is light*   A m_____ u____ m_t_____ p_____ e_ l_____

e. *New products are very expensive*   L__ p_____ n_____ s___ m__ c___

f. *We can pay online and contactless*   P_____ p_____ e_ l_____ y s___ c_____

g. *It is light and easy to transport*   E_ l_____ y f_____ d_ t_____

h. *It is vital for our daily chores*   E_ v_____ p___ n_____ t_____ d_____

i. *Mobile technology is attractive because it's multifunctional*
L_ t_____ m_____ e_ a_____ p_____ e_ m_____

22. Translate the following sentences into Spanish

a. I like to use my laptop because it's easy to travel with it

b. Nowadays, mobile technology is everywhere (omnipresent) in our lives

c. I always use my smartwatch because it's efficient and compact

d. One of the disadvantages of mobile technology is that it causes a lot of distractions

e. One of the advantages of mobile technology is geographical flexibility

f. I love my mobile phone because it is practical

g. From now on, mobile technology is indispensable in the world of work

h. It's fast and entertaining, but also practical to communicate with my friends and my family

23. Guided composition write five short paragraphs about mobile technology. Say the following things

- Introduce yourself (5 details)
- Say how you use mobile technology in your daily life (4 details)
- Talk about the advantages of mobile technology (4 details)
- Mention the disadvantages of mobile technology (2 details)
- Say how you use social media

Key questions

¿Qué piensas sobre las tecnología móvil de hoy en día?	*What do you think about mobile technology nowadays?*
¿Cómo usas la tecnología móvil en tu vida diaria?	*How do you use mobile technology in your daily life?*
¿Por qué te gusta usar tu portátil?	*Why do you like using your laptop?*
¿Cuáles son las ventajas de la tecnología móvil?	*What are the advantages of mobile technology?*
¿Cuáles son las desventajas de la tecnología móvil? Justifica tu respuesta.	*What are the disadvantages of mobile technology? Justify your answer.*
Por lo general, ¿para qué utilizas la tecnología móvil?	*Generally, what do you use mobile technology to do?*
¿Crees que la tecnología móvil ha cambiado la manera en que trabajamos? ¿Cómo?	*Do you think mobile technology has changed the way we work? How?*
¿Crees que la tecnología móvil ha transformado la manera en que vivimos?	*Do you believe that mobile technology has transformed the way we live?*

Unit 3. Mobile technology (past tense)

Desde hace unos años, *For some years now,* **Desde hace tiempo,** *For some time,* **En los últimos años,** *In the last few years,* **Recientemente,** *Recently,*	**la tecnología móvil se ha vuelto** *mobile technology has become*	**atractiva debido a su versatilidad** *attractive due to its versatility* **esencial para nuestro entretenimiento** *essential for our entertainment* **indispensable para viajar** *indispensable for travelling* **vital para nuestras tareas cotidianas** *vital for our daily tasks*

Anteayer, *The day before yesterday,* **Ayer por la noche,** *Yesterday evening,* **Hace dos días,** *Two days ago,* **El pasado sábado,** *Last Saturday,*	**jugué con** *I played on* **usé mucho** *I used a lot* **utilicé** *I used* **trabajé desde** *I worked on*	**mi altavoz portátil** *my portable speaker* **mi ordenador portátil** *my laptop* **mi reloj inteligente** *my smartwatch* **mi tablet** *my tablet* **mi teléfono móvil** *my mobile phone*	**para** *(in order) to*	**escuchar música** *listen to music* **hablar con mis amigos por WhatsApp** *talk to my friends on WhatsApp* **leer un artículo** *read an article* **subir fotos** *upload photos* **ver una película** *see a film*

Además, usé mi tablet/teléfono móvil *Furthermore, I used my tablet/phone*	**para**	**acceder a aplicaciones modernas para hacer los deberes** *access modern apps to do my homework* **comprar cosas en internet** *buy things on the internet* **comunicarme fuera del trabajo sin problemas** *communicate out of the office without any problem* **trabajar desde casa** *work from home*

Hace unos días *A few days ago,* **La semana pasada** *Last week,*	**gasté mis ahorros** *I spent my savings* **gasté mucho dinero** *I spent a lot of money*	**en una tablet de última generación** *on a next generation tablet* **para comprar un teléfono móvil nuevo** *to buy a new mobile phone*

Ayer por la noche *Yesterday evening,* **El fin de semana pasado** *Last weekend,*	**malgasté mucho tiempo** *I wasted a lot of time* **perdí por lo menos dos horas** *I lost at least two hours*	**en mis redes sociales** **usando mi teléfono** **viendo *chorradas**	*on my social media* *distractions on my phone* *looking at nonsense*

---

*Authors note *"Una chorrada"* is a more idiomatic/informal word for *"tontería"* – a silly thing

1. Phrase puzzle

a. unos Desde años hace   *For some years now*

b. artículo un Leer   *To read an article*

c. ahorros mis Gasté   *I spent my savings*

d. remota Pagar de forma   *To pay remotely*

e. problema Sin   *Without any problem*

f. horas Perdí dos   *I lost two hours*

g. chorradas viendo   *Watching stupid things*

h. WhatsApp por Hablar   *Talk on WhatsApp*

i. mis Para deberes   *For my homework*

j. La pasada semana   *Last week*

k. diarias tareas Nuestras   *Our daily tasks*

l. un Para móvil comprar nuevo   *To buy a new phone*

2. Complete

a. Comprar ____ en línea   *Buy things online*

b. Pagar __ forma remota   *To pay remotely*

c. _____ el móvil   *I used my phone*

d. _____ el tiempo   *I wasted my time*

e. _____ dos horas   *I lost two hours*

f. _____ dos días   *Two days ago*

g. La semana _____   *Last week*

h. Hace _____ días   *A few days ago*

i. _____ con   *I played with/on*

j. Ayer ___ la mañana   *Yesterday morning*

k. Mi tablet _____   *My new tablet*

3. Turn the following verbs into the preterite *(pretérito indefinido)* tense and then translate into English

Present	Preterite tense	English Translation
Uso		
Trabajo		
Gasto		
Pierdo		
Malgasto		
Juego		
Utilizo		
Puedo		
Tomo		

4. Correct the wrong spellings

a. Malogasté mi tiempo

b. Jugé con mi tablet

c. Gassté mucho dinero

d. Gasté todos (*all*) mis aoros

e. Fue rapidó y divirtido

f. Pude comunicame

g. Desde haga tiempo

h. Por lo mens dos horas

i. Móvil de la primero generación

j. Mi jerol inteligente

k. En los ultimes años

5. Circle the correct verb for each sentence

a. **Utilicé/tomé/gasté** mi portátil en el avión

b. **Gasté/trabajé/usé** mucho dinero en las compras en línea

c. **Jugé/perdí/pude** comunicarme fuera de la oficina

d. **Malgasté/trabajé/dormí** desde mi portátil

e. **Logré/usé/compré** acceder a aplicaciones modernas

6. Add the missing accents

a. Use mi telefono movil

b. Gaste mucho dinero en mi reloj inteligente

c. Trabaje desde mi tablet y lei un articulo

d. Perdi dos horas en un portatil de ultima generacion

Conversación entre amigos (Part 1)

Rosario: ¿Cómo ha cambiado la tecnología móvil tu vida cotidiana?

Víctor: Diría que *[I would say]* gracias a la tecnología móvil mi vida es más sencilla y agradable. Por ejemplo, el fin de semana pasado volé a Barcelona y trabajé en mi portátil durante el vuelo. Leí unos artículos y vi noticias en un canal de YouTube. También usé mi teléfono móvil para contestar mis mensajes y para entrar en las redes sociales. Antes de la tecnología móvil, esto no era posible. Me gusta viajar con mi portátil porque es muy ligero y práctico.

Rosario: ¿Cuáles crees que son las ventajas de la tecnología móvil?

Víctor: Viajo mucho por mi trabajo y por eso para mí es muy conveniente. Ayer pude comunicarme con mis colegas mientras estaba fuera de la oficina. Esto me permitió trabajar de forma remota sin ningún problema. Me acostumbré a trabajar desde casa durante la pandemia del coronavirus y fue posible gracias a los últimos avances tecnológicos en materia de comunicación. Hice todas mis reuniones en Zoom y también conocí a mis clientes así.

Rosario: ¿Últimamente has utilizado tu portátil para tus actividades de ocio? ¿Cómo?

Víctor: ¡Sí, por supuesto! Ayer usé mi portátil para jugar a videojuegos en línea y también para ver películas en Netflix. Asimismo, usé mi teléfono móvil para enviar mensajes a mis amigos, sacar fotos, escuchar música y leer las noticias. Esto me encantó, porque era muy práctico y entretenido al mismo tiempo.

7. Match

Agradable	Possible
Fácil	I worked
El vuelo	Remote working
Antes	To read
Posible	At the same time
Trabajé	The flight
Viajar	Far
Teletrabajar	Pleasant
Al mismo tiempo	To travel
Lejos	Easy
Leer	Before

8. Spot and fix the wrong translations

a. Diría que — *I would like to*

b. Viajo mucho — *I never travel*

c. Mis compañeros — *My schools*

d. Lejos de la oficina — *Near the office*

e. Fui — *I ate*

f. Trabajé — *I travelled*

g. Es posible — *It was possible*

h. Enviar mensajes — *To receive messages*

i. Escuchar música — *To download music*

j. Entretenido — *Tedious*

9. Complete the translation from the first question and answer above

Q: How has mobile technology changed your daily life?

A: I would _____ that thanks to mobile _____ my life is more simple and _____. For example, last weekend I _____ to Barcelona and worked on my laptop _____ the flight. I read some _____ and watched news on a YouTube channel. I also _____ my mobile phone to reply to my messages and to access _____ networks. _____ mobile technology existed, this was not _____.

10. Circle the correct English translation

	1	2	3
Avión	Boat	Plane	Car
Ligero	Heavy	Loud	Light
Fui	I went	I gave	I took
Enviar	To receive	To send	To bring
Entretenido	Boring	Interesting	Entertaining

11. Complete choosing the appropriate missing verb from the options below

a. La semana pasada _____ a Barcelona

b. _____ mi teléfono móvil bastante a menudo

c. _____ que mi vida es más sencilla y agradable

d. Al final, me _____ a trabajar desde casa

e. Es posible _____ a los avances tecnológicos

f. _____ todas mis reuniones en Zoom y conocí a mis clientes

g. Me _____ porque era muy práctico y divertido

h. Antes de la tecnología móvil, esto no ___ posible.

diría	usé	gracias	gustó
acostumbré	era	hice	volé

12. True, False or Not mentioned?

a. Because of mobile technology, Víctor's life is now more difficult

b. Last weekend he took a plane to Madrid

c. He worked on his laptop during the flight

d. He travels a lot for his work

e. Thanks to mobile technology, he can communicate with his colleagues remotely

f. He has never worked from home

g. He knows how to use Zoom

h. He also uses his laptop to play video games

i. Yesterday, he used his mobile phone to take some photos

13. Answer the following questions about the conversation above

a. Why does Víctor like to travel with his laptop? (2 details)

b. Where did he go last weekend?

c. Explain in your own words what "teletrabajar" means

d. How did Víctor meet his client during the pandemic?

e. What did he do on his laptop during his free time yesterday? (2 details)

f. Please list the 4 things he did on his mobile phone yesterday

-

-

-

-

THE LANGUAGE GYM

Conversación entre amigos (Part 2)

Rosario: En tu opinión, ¿cuáles son las desventajas de la tecnología móvil? Explica, por favor.

Víctor: Como en todo, hay puntos fuertes y débiles *[strong and weak points]*. Yo diría que el mayor punto débil de la tecnología móvil es, ante todo, su precio. Estos productos son muy caros y no están al alcance *[within reach]* de todos. Por semana, la semana pasada gasté mucho dinero (todos mis ahorros) para comprar mi nueva tablet.

En segundo lugar, mucha gente se vuelve adicta a sus teléfonos móviles y me parece una pena, porque hay menos conversaciones cara a cara y relaciones directas. También es una gran distracción. Anoche, yo mismo *[I myself]* perdí al menos dos horas debido a distracciones en mi teléfono.

Rosario: ¿Crees que la tecnología móvil ha transformado la forma en que vivimos?

Víctor: Sí, sin duda. En los últimos años la tecnología móvil se ha vuelto indispensable tanto en el mundo laboral como en el hogar. Estos dispositivos electrónicos portátiles están omnipresentes en nuestras vidas.

Rosario: Además de tu teléfono y el portátil, ¿qué otros dispositivos usas y cómo?

Víctor: Ayer por la mañana, por ejemplo, usé mi reloj inteligente cuando hice deporte para saber cuánto pasos hice. Salí a correr y pude leer mis mensajes y ver mis notificaciones.

Rosario: ¿Cuál es tu dispositivo electrónico favorito?

Víctor: Ya no viajo sin mi altavoz portátil, porque me gusta escuchar mi música favorita, vaya donde vaya. Es muy compacto, ligero y eficaz. ¡La calidad del sonido es excelente!

14. Positive or Negative?

a. El mayor punto débil de la tecnología es, ante todo, su precio.

b. Estos productos son muy caros y no están al alcance de todos

c. Es compacto, ligero y eficaz

d. Perdí por lo menos dos horas

e. ¡La calidad del sonido es excelente!

f. Mucha gente se vuelve adicta a sus teléfonos móviles

g. Salí a correr y pude leer mis mensajes y ver mis notificaciones.

h. La semana pasada gasté mucho dinero por mi nueva tablet.

15. Faulty translation: correct the translation mistakes below

a. Omnipresente	*Practical*
b. Indispensable	*Available*
c. Débil	*Strong*
d. Adicto	*A dictaphone*
e. Muy caro	*Very cheap*
f. Me parece una pena	*I find that amazing*
g. Dispositivo electrónico	*Electric device*
h. Pude leer	*I was able to write*
i. Mis mensajes	*My messengers*

16. Complete the translation from the first question and answer above

Q: In your _____ , what are the _____ of mobile technology? Please _____ .

A: As with _____ , there are some _____ points and some _____ points. I would _____ that the _____ weakness of mobile technology is, _____ all, its _____ . These products are very _____ and are not accessible to _____ . For example, last _____ , I _____ a lot of _____ (all my _____) in order to buy my _____ tablet.

17. Find the Spanish for the following words or sentences in the conversation above

a. Firstly

b. Secondly

c. Last week

d. I went out for a run

e. My smartwatch

f. I spent a lot of money

g. I find it a shame

h. It is very compact, light and efficient

i. I was able to read my messages

j. They are omnipresent in our lives

18. Answer the following questions about the conversation above

a. What is the first weakness Víctor mentions about mobile technology?

b. What is the second weak point?

c. What mobile device did he use to exercise yesterday?

d. What is his favourite electronic device and why?

e. What did he buy last week?

f. What was he able to do while jogging?

g. What two adjectives does he use to describe his portable speaker?

h. How much time did he lose yesterday because of his mobile phone?

19. Complete choosing the appropriate missing words from the options below

En los últimos años, la tecnología móvil se ha _____ indispensable tanto en el mundo del _____ como en casa. Estos dispositivos electrónicos portátiles están _____ en nuestras vidas.

Ayer por la _____, por ejemplo, _____ mi _____ inteligente para hacer deporte porque es _____ y compacto. _____ a correr y pude leer mis mensajes y ver mis _____.

Ya no viajo sin mi _____ portátil, porque me gusta escuchar mi música favorita, vaya donde _____. Es muy pequeño, pero la calidad del _____ es excelente.

mañana	eficaz	reloj	trabajo
notificaciones	vuelto	salí	altavoz
usé	vaya	sonido	omnipresentes

20. Translate into Spanish

a. I was able to read

b. I like to listen to my favourite music

c. I went jogging

d. I find that unfortunate

e. I spent a lot of money

f. I used my smartwatch

g. I lost at least two hours

h. I never travel without my portable speaker anymore

21. Answer the following questions to the best of your ability using the Sentence Builder from this unit and the conversation above for support. Then practice with a partner

a. ¿Qué ha cambiado la tecnología móvil en tu vida?

b. ¿Cuáles son las desventajas de la tecnología móvil? Justifica tu respuesta.

c. ¿Has usado tu ordenador portátil para tus pasatiempos recientemente? ¿Cómo?

d. ¿Cuál es tu dispositivo electrónico favorito? ¿Por qué?

Key questions

¿Cómo ha cambiado tu vida la tecnología móvil?	*How has mobile technology changed your life?*
Cuéntame cómo usaste la tecnología móvil ayer.	*Tell me how you have used mobile technology yesterday.*
¿Has usado tu ordenador portátil para tus pasatiempos recientemente? ¿Cómo?	*Have you used your laptop for your leisure activities recently? How?*
¿Cuáles son las ventajas de la tecnología móvil?	*What are the advantages of mobile technology?*
¿Cuáles son las desventajas de la tecnología móvil? Justifica tu respuesta.	*What are the disadvantages of mobile technology? Justify your answer.*
¿Por qué razones usas normalmente la tecnología móvil?	*For what reasons do you generally use mobile technology?*
¿Piensas que la tecnología móvil ha cambiado la manera en que trabajamos? ¿Cómo?	*Do you think mobile technology has changed the way we work? If yes, how?*
¿Piensas que la tecnología móvil ha cambiado la manera en que vivimos?	*Do you believe that mobile technology has transformed the way we live?*
Dame algunos ejemplos de cómo has usado la tecnología móvil para hacer deberes esta semana.	*Give me some examples of how you have used mobile technology for your homework this week.*

Unit 4. Pros and cons of new technologies (present tense)

		fomentan la creatividad *encourage creativity*	
Me gustan (mucho) *I like (a lot)*		me hacen ahorrar tiempo *save me time*	
		simplifican la vida cotidiana *simplify everyday life*	
		son una manera de divertirse *are a way to entertain oneself*	
	las nuevas tecnologías porque *new technologies because they*	**me ayudan a** *they help me to* **nos ayudan a** *they help us to*	**buscar información** *find information more easily* **ser más productivo/a/os/as** *be more productive* **estar mejor organizado/a/os/as** *be better organised*
Me encantan *I love*			
Estoy a favor de *I am in favour of*		**me permiten** *they allow me to* **nos permiten** *they allow us to*	**acceder a una gran cantidad de información** *(to) access a great amount of information* **comunicarnos de forma gratuita e instantánea** *(to) communicate freely and instantly* **hacer las cosas más rápido** *(to) do things faster*

		afectan de forma negativa las relaciones personales *affect negatively personal relationships*
Odio *I hate*		aumentan los riesgos de seguridad en línea *increase security risks online*
		causan muchas distracciones *cause many distractions*
No me gustan nada *I don't like at all*	**las nuevas tecnologías porque** *new technologies because they*	nos hacen desconectarnos de la realidad *make us disconnect from reality*
		nos hacen perder el tiempo *make us waste time*
Estoy en contra de *I am against*		nos hacen perezosos *make us lazy*
		pueden llevar a la pérdida de datos *can lead to data losses*
		son caras y por lo tanto no accesibles para todos *are expensive and therefore not accessible for all*

THE LANGUAGE GYM

1. Match

Dar acceso	*To do things faster*
Fomentar la creatividad	*To increase productivity*
Buscar información	*To simplify everyday life*
Ahorrar tiempo	*To look for information*
Hacer las cosas más rápido	*To allow better organisation*
Permitir mejor organización	*To reduce efforts*
Divertirse	*To give access*
Comunicarse de forma gratuita	*To encourage creativity*
Reducir el esfuerzo	*To have fun*
Simplificar la vida cotidiana	*To communicate for free*
Aumentar la productividad	*To save time*

2. Find the Spanish for the following in activity 1

a. *Access*   A _ _ _ _ _

b. *To reduce*   R _ _ _ _ _ _

c. *Life*   L _ v _ _ _

d. *To give*   D _ _

e. *Things*   C _ _ _ _

f. *Time*   T _ _ _ _ _

g. *To save*   A _ _ _ _ _ _

h. *Better*   M _ _ _ _

i. *Faster*   M _ _ r _ _ _ _ _

j. *To have fun* D _ _ _ _ _ _ _ _

3. Complete choosing the appropriate missing word from the options below

La nuevas tecnologías…

a. …nos _____ hacer las cosas más rapido

b. …nos ayudan a estar _____ organizados

c. …nos hacen _____

d. …_____ los riesgos de seguridad en línea

e. …fomentan la _____

f. …afectan de _____ negativa las relaciones personales

g. …nos _____ a buscar información

h. … son caras y por lo _____ no son accesibles para todos

aumentan	perezosos	tanto	ayudan
permiten	forma	creatividad	mejor

4. Translate into English

a. Dan acceso   *They _____*

b. Son   *They _____*

c. Permiten   *They _____*

d. Simplifican *They _____*

e. Aumentan   *They _____*

f. Reducen   *They _____*

g. Desconectan *They _____*

h. Fomentan   *They _____*

i. Afectan   *They _____*

5. Broken words

a. Más prod_ _ _ _vo   *More productive*

b. Una ma _ _ra de divert _ _ _e *A way to have fun*

c. La vi_a co_ _ _iana   *Everyday life*

d. Las nuevas te_ _ _ _ _ _ _as   *New technologies*

e. Pér_ _ _ _ de datos   *Data losses*

f. Muc_ _s distr_ _ _ _ _nes   *Many distractions*

g. Rie_ _os de seguri_ _d   *Security risks*

6. Anagrams

a. oejMr   *Better*   g. roP ol natto *Therefore*

b. nE tcnroa *Against*   h. nIentatásna *Instant*

c. Prrdee   *To waste*   i. iRgseo   *Risk*

d. aUn mrneaa *A way*   j. diaV   *Life*

e. A vaorf   *In favour* k. Croa   *Expensive*

f. aériPdd   *Loss*   l. Pzeeorso   *Lazy*

7. Sentence puzzle

a. Las tecnologías nuevas permiten nos productividad aumentar la
New technologies allow us to increase productivity

b. nuevas Las tecnologías nos hacer las permiten más cosas rápido
New technologies allow us to do things faster

c. nuevas negativa tecnologías afectan forma las Las relaciones personales de
New technologies negatively affect personal relationships

d. Las perezosos nuevas hacen tecnologías nos
New technologies make us lazy

e. tecnologías Me ahorrar encantan las ayudan nuevas porque nos a tiempo
I love new technologies because they make us save time

f. fomentan Estoy las a favor de nuevas tecnologías porque la creatividad
I am in favour of new technologies because they encourage creativity

g. Estoy nuevas en el hacen contra de las tecnologías porque nos perder el tiempo
I am against new technologies because they make me waste time

8. Spot and write in the missing word: one word is missing from each sentence

Las nuevas tecnologías…

a. … hacen ahorrar tiempo

b. … aumentan riesgos de seguridad en línea

c. … simplifican vida cotidiana

d. … son caras y lo tanto no son accesibles para todos

e. … nos permiten acceder a una gran de información

f. … nos perezosos

9. Spot the error and correct it

a. Pueden lavar a la pérdida de datos

b. Son un manera de divertirse

c. Nos ayudan a ser mejor organizados

d. Causan muchas distractions

e. Sos hacen perezosos

f. No son accessibles para todos

g. Nos ayudan a ahorrar tempo

h. Nos hacen desconectar la realidad

10. Complete with the appropriate verb

a. Las nuevas tecnologías a_ _ _ _ _ _ de forma negativa las relaciones personales

b. Me encantan las nuevas tecnologías porque me a_ _ _ _ _ a ser más productiva

c. Estoy a favor de las nuevas tecnologías porque s_ _ _ _ _ _ _ _ _ _ la vida cotidiana

d. Nos p_ _ _ _ _ _ _ comunicarnos de forma gratuita e instantánea

e. Odio las nuevas tecnologías porque me h_ _ _ _ perder el tiempo

f. Por otro lado me ayudan a b_ _ _ _ _ información

g. Igualmente que me hacen a_ _ _ _ _ _ tiempo porque son rápidas y eficaces

h. Lo más importante para mí es que me a_ _ _ _ _ a estar más organizado y me p_ _ _ _ _ _ _ hacer las cosas más rápido

11. Circle the correct translation

		1	2	3
a.	La vida	Envy	Life	Risk
b.	El tiempo	Thing	Day	Time
c.	Las cosas	Things	People	Gadgets
d.	Aumentar	To Reduce	To Increase	To Affect
e.	Más rápido	Worse	Slower	Faster
f.	Perder	To lose/waste	To make/do	To change/modify
g.	Afectar	To infect	To give	To affect
h.	En contra	Against	In favour	Opposite
i.	Abrir	To close	To open	To give

12. Guided translation

a. *Personal relationships*   L _ _ r _ _ _ _ _ _ _ _ _   p _ _ _ _ _ _ _ _

b. *To be better organised*   E _ _ _ _ m _ _ _ _ o _ _ _ _ _ _ _ _

c. *The security risks*   L _ _ r _ _ _ _ _ _ d _ s _ _ _ _ _ _ _

d. *To waste time*   P _ _ _ _ _ e _ t _ _ _ _ _

e. *They cause a lot of distractions*   C _ _ _ _ _ m _ _ _ _ _ d _ _ _ _ _ _ _ _ _ _ _

f. *They help to look for information*   A _ _ _ _ _ a b _ _ _ _ _ i _ _ _ _ _ _ _ _

g. *They simplify everyday life*   S _ _ _ _ _ _ _ _ _ l _ v _ _ c _ _ _ _ _ _ _

h. *To do things faster*   H _ _ _ _ l _ _ c _ _ _ _ m _ _ r _ _ _ _ _

13. Translate into Spanish

a. I love new technologies because they allow us to increase our productivity

b. Moreover, they simplify everyday life because they allow us to do things faster

c. Likewise, they encourage creativity…

d. …and are a way to entertain oneself

e. Unfortunately, they cause a lot of distractions

f. Therefore, sometimes they make me waste time

g. Moreover, they disconnect us from reality and often negatively affect personal relationships

h. There are also many dangers. For instance, they can lead to data losses

i. However, I am against new technologies because they make us lazy and disconnect us from reality

TEXT 1 – Raúl (15 años, Pamplona)

(1) Desde mi punto de vista, las nuevas tecnologías tienen ventajas e inconvenientes. Lo que me encanta, es que nos permiten acceder a una gran cantidad de información con solo unos clics. Siempre uso internet para buscar información para mi trabajo escolar o cuando necesito encontrar la ubicación *[location]* de un lugar o una tienda, información sobre un producto u horarios de un negocio. Internet te da acceso fácil a una gran variedad de documentos y sitios web de toda clase, lo cual es muy práctico.

(2) También me gustan mucho las nuevas tecnologías, porque creo que fomentan la creatividad, gracias a las numerosas aplicaciones ingeniosas para dibujar, tomar y editar fotos, y también grabar y editar vídeos. Las actividades creativas que antes necesitaban un nivel elevado de competencia técnica, están ahora al alcance de cualquiera *[within anyone's reach]*. Hay muchos tutoriales disponibles en la red de manera gratuita, que nos sirven cuando queremos aprender a usarlas.

(3) Sin embargo, lo que odio, es que las nuevas tecnologías afectan negativamente a las relaciones personales. Debido a la mensajería instantánea y a los correos electrónicos, la gente no se habla tanto cara a cara y esto puede desarrollar una sensación de aislamiento en algunas personas. Por otra parte, estoy en contra de las nuevas teconologías ya que causan muchas distracciones de la vida cotidiana y pueden llevar a comportamientos obsesivos, sobre todo con las redes sociales.

(4) Otro gran problema ligado a las nuevas tecnologías es su vulnerabilidad en cuanto a la seguridad en línea. Cada día, muchas personas son víctimas de diversos fraudes en línea. Las filtraciones *[leaks]* de datos bancarios o personales ocurren con mucha frecuencia y, lamentablemente, la piratería se ha convertido en la profesión de los delincuentes modernos que se aprovechan de posibles defectos en los sistemas informáticos.

14. Find the Spanish equivalent for the following words/phrases in paragraph 1

a. From my point of view

b. They allow us to access

c. For my schoolwork

d. I need

e. Timetables

f. Business

g. Range/variety

h. Of all kinds

15. Faulty translation: correct the 8 translation mistakes in the translation of paragraph 2 below

I also like new technologies a bit because in my opinion they encourage creativity thanks to a few ingenious apps to draw, copy and edit photos and also for recording and editing photos. The creative activities which before required a low level of technical skills, are now within noone's reach. There are many free tutors available online which are useful when we want to learn to sell them.

16. Complete the sentences below based on paragraphs 3 and 4

a. New technologies negatively affect _____ _____

b. Because of instant messaging and emails, people _____

c. Raúl is against new technologies because _____ _____

d. They can also lead to _____

e. Another big problem is vulnerability _____ _____

f. Every day, many people are victims of _____ _____

g. Leaks of banking data _____

h. Possible flaws _____

TEXT 2 – Beatríz (17 años, Huelva)

(1) En mi opinión, las nuevas tecnologías tienen cosas buenas y malas. En general, estoy a favor de estos dispositivos electrónicos porque han revolucionado totalmente nuestras vidas y la forma en que trabajamos y nos comunicamos hoy. Lo que más me gusta es que facilitan la búsqueda de información y nos permiten hacer las cosas más rápido. Siempre uso mi ordenador para hacer mis deberes, porque gracias a internet tengo acceso a mucha información muy rápidamente, lo que me ahorra tiempo.

(2) Además, uso mi teléfono móvil todo el tiempo para mantenerme en contacto con mis amigos y parientes. Las aplicaciones de mensajes instantáneos, como Whatsapp, son muy rápidas y convenientes. Además son gratuitas y funcionan de un país a otro. También uso mi tablet para entretenerme. Me gusta jugar a videojuegos en línea y también ver mis series favoritas en Netflix. Asimismo, paso algo de tiempo en las redes sociales todos los días y me encanta publicar fotos y vídeos en Instagram.

(3) Por otro lado, uno de los puntos negativos de las nuevas tecnologías son las distracciones que generan, y todo el mundo lo sabe. Por un lado nos ayudan a ahorrar tiempo en el trabajo, pero por otro nos pueden hacer perder mucho tiempo, sobre todo por culpa de las redes sociales. Las notificaciones tienden a distraernos constantemente si se dejan encendidas y se vuelve difícil concentrarnos en otras cosas. Muchas personas se vuelven adictas a las redes sociales y pasan la mayor parte de su tiempo allí.

(4) Asimismo, lo que me preocupa es el jaqueo y la inseguridad que traen estos nuevos dispositivos. El robo de datos, el fraude de identidad y los sistemas informáticos son vulnerables y pueden poner en peligro nuestra información personal, así como nuestros datos bancarios. Recientemente, a mi papá le clonaron su tarjeta de crédito y le robaron mucho dinero de su cuenta. ¡Qué pena!

17. Find the Spanish equivalent for the following words in paragraph 1

a. *New (plural feminine)*   N_ _ _ _ _

b. *Good (plural feminine)*   B_ _ _ _ _

c. *Bad (plural feminine)*   M_ _ _ _

d. *Lives*   V_ _ _ _

e. *Way*   F_ _ _ _

f. *Our (plural feminine)*   N_ _ _ _ _ _ _

g. *(They) Make easy*   F_ _ _ _ _ _ _ _

h. *(They) Allow*   P_ _ _ _ _ _

i. *Quickly*   R_ _ _ _ _ _ _ _ _

j. *Time*   T_ _ _ _ _

18. Complete the following sentences based on paragraph 2

a. I use my mobile phone all the time to _____ _____

b. Instant messaging apps, such as _____ are very _____ and _____

c. Moreover, they are_____ and _____

d. I also use my tablet to _____.
I like to _____ online and also _____ series on Netflix

e. Likewise, I spend a bit of time on _____ _____ every day and I love to _____ and _____ on Instagram

19. Translate into English the following items from paragraph 4

a. Fraude de identidad

b. La inseguridad que traen

c. Los sistemas informáticos son vulnerables

d. Pueden poner en peligro nuestra información personal

e. Nuestros datos bancarios

f. Recientemente

g. Le robaron mucho dinero

h. ¡Qué pena!

20. Complete the text with the missing verbs choosing from the options below

En mi opinión, las nuevas tecnologías _____ tanto positivas como negativas. Lo que me encanta es que con solo un par de *clicks* del ratón te _____ acceder a mucha información. Entonces, siempre _____ internet para buscar información para mi trabajo escolar o cuando _____ información sobre un lugar, una tienda, una marca, horarios o una persona. Internet _____ fácil acceso a una amplia gama de documentos y sitios de todo tipo, lo cual _____ muy práctico.

Desde otro punto de vista, uno de los puntos _____ de las nuevas tecnologías es que _____ distracciones, y eso lo sabe todo el mundo. Por un lado, nos _____ a ahorrar tiempo en el trabajo, pero por otro lado, también _____ mucho tiempo, especialmente debido a las redes sociales. Las notificaciones tienden a distraernos constantemente si se dejan _____ y se vuelve difícil concentrarnos en otra cosa. Muchas personas _____ adictas a las redes sociales y pasan la mayor parte de su tiempo allí.

crean	da	permiten	activadas	necesito	son
se vuelven	uso	negativos	es	perdemos	ayudan

21. Translate into English

a. Las nuevas tecnologías son tanto positivas como negativas.

b. Estoy a favor de las nuevas tecnologías.

c. Han revolucionado completamente nuestras vidas.

d. Lo que me gusta es que nos permiten hacer las cosas más rápido.

e. Las notificaciones de las redes sociales tienden a distraernos constantemente.

f. Muchas personas se vuelven adictas a las redes sociales.

g. Lo que más me preocupa es el jaqueo.

h. El robo de datos puede poner en peligro nuestra información personal.

i. Los delincuentes modernos se aprovechan de los fallos en los sistemas informáticos.

22. Complete with the missing vowels

a. _l j_qu_ _   *Computer hacking*

b. D_str_cc__n   *Distraction*

c. _d_ct_   *Addicted*

d. D_sp_s_t_v_s   *Devices*

e. _st_y _ f_v_r   *I am in favour*

f. R_b_ d_ d_t_s   *Data theft*

g. _pl_c_c__n_s d_ m_ns_j_r__   *Messaging apps*

h. T_nt_ p_s_t_v_s c_m_ n_g_t_v_s
Positive as much as negative

23. Anagrams

a. *People*   nGeet

b. *Thefts*   obsoR

c. *Devices*   iDtsosiiopvs

d. *Hacking*   oJqaue

e. *Addicted*   icAtod

f. *Good*   Bnuoe

g. *Bad (pl)*   Mlosa

h. *Identity*   nIetiaddd

i. *Notifications*   iontfcieacNios

24. Translate into Spanish (word level)

a. *Hacking:* J	h. *To save:* A	o. *Criminals:* D
b. *Negative:* N	i. *Life:* V	p. *Thefts:* R
c. *Positive:* P	j. *Addicted:* A	q. *Time:* T
d. *Fast:* R	k. *Data:* D	r. *Electronic:* E
e. *Things:* C	l. *Devices:* D	s. *(They) Become:* S
f. *Systems:* S	m. *People:* G	t. *Tablet:* T
g. *Fraud:* F	n. *Against:* E c	u. *Computer:* O

25. Translate into Spanish (phrase level)

a. Computer hacking	h. Pros and cons
b. Data theft	i. Faster
c. Credit card	j. To become addicted
d. In favour	k. Electronic devices
e. IT systems	l. Data loss
f. To waste time	m. Social media
g. To save time	n. The way we work

26. Translate into Spanish

a. I love new technologies because they allow us to increase our productivity.

b. Moreover, they simplify our daily life because they allow us to do things faster.

c. New technologies also encourage creativity and are a good way to entertain oneself.

d. Unfortunately, many times they make us waste time. For instance, social media notifications often make us lose our concentration.

e. Moreover, they disconnect us from reality and often negatively affect personal relationships.

f. They also make us lazy because we can do everything from home.

g. There are also many dangers. For instance, there are many identity thefts and data thefts. Last week, my father had his credit card cloned.

27. Write a 140 words composition in which you include the following points

- What electronic devices you have and how you use them
- What social media you use and why
- What are the pros and cons of new technologies as far as you are concerned
- The pros and cons of new technologies for people in general
- What you like the most about them
- What you like the least about them

Key questions

Según tú, ¿cuáles son los aspectos positivos de las nuevas tecnologías?	*According to you, what are the positive aspects of new technologies?*
En tu opinión, ¿cuáles son los aspectos negativos?	*In your opinion, what are their negative aspects?*
Dame un ejemplo de cómo las nuevas tecnologías mejoran tu vida diaria.	*Give me an example of how new technologies improve your daily life.*
¿Estás a favor o en contra de las nuevas tecnologías?	*Are you in favour or against new technologies?*
¿Has sido alguna vez víctima de un fraude en internet?	*Have you ever been a victim of fraud on the internet?*
Dame un ejemplo de cómo los dispositivos electrónicos te ahorran tiempo.	*Give me an example of how electronic devices make you save time.*
Ahora, da un ejemplo de cómo los dispositivos electrónicos te hacen perder el tiempo.	*Now, give an example of how electronic devices make you waste time.*

Unit 4. Pros and cons of new technologies (past tense)

Desde pequeño/a *Since I was little* **Desde que tenía 'x' años** *Since I was 'x' years old* **Siempre** *Always*	**he tenido un ordenador portátil** *I have had a laptop* **he tenido un teléfono móvil** *I have had a mobile phone* **he usado internet** *I have used internet*	**y lo bueno es que me ha ayudado a** *and the good thing is that it has helped me*	**ahorrar tiempo** *to save time* **aumentar mi productividad** *to increase my productivity* **buscar información** *to search for information* **comunicarme de forma más instantánea** *to communicate more instantly* **divertirme en mi tiempo libre** *to have fun in my free time* **hacer las cosas más rápido** *to do things faster* **hacer nuevos amigos con pasatiempos similares** *to make new friends with similar hobbies* **organizarme mejor** *to organise myself better* **simplificar mi día a día** *to simplify my everyday life* **tener acceso a mucha información** *to have access to a lot of information*

Sin embargo, *However,*	**lo malo de internet es que ha** *the bad thing about internet is that it has*	**afectado negativamente las relaciones personales** *negatively affected personal relationships* **aumentado los peligros en línea** *increased online dangers* **causado muchas distracciones** *caused many distractions* **facilitado el ciberacoso** *facilitated cyberbullying*
	lo malo de internet es que <u>nos</u> ha *the bad thing about internet is that it has*	**desconectado de la realidad** *disconnected <u>us</u> from reality* **hecho más perezosos** *made <u>us</u> lazier* **hecho perder el tiempo** *made <u>us</u> waste time*

1. Match

Desde pequeño	*However*
Me ha ayudado	*It has caused distractions*
Simplificar	*The good thing is*
Sin embargo	*The bad thing about internet*
Lo bueno es	*It has made us lazier*
Desde que tenía 'x' años	*I've had a mobile phone*
Lo malo de internet	*To simplify*
Nos ha hecho más perezosos	*Since I was little*
Ha causado distracciones	*Since I was 'x' years old*
He tenido un móvil	*It has helped me*

2. Complete with the missing letters, then translate into English

a. Desde que t _ _ _ _ 'x' años

b. Des _ _ _ _ _ _ do de la realidad

c. He t _ _ _ _ _ un portátil

d. Lo m _ _ _ de in _ _ _ _ _ _ es

e. Faci _ _ _ _ _ n la comunicación

f. Simp _ _ _ _ _ _ r mi día a d _ _

g. Pe _ _ _ _ el tiempo

h. S _ _ emb _ r _ o

i. Ha aum _ _ _ _ _ _ los peligros

j. Ha facilitado el c _ _ _ _ _ c _ _ o

3. Write the Spanish past participle for the following verbs

e.g. Perder	Perdido
Buscar	
Afectar	
Causar	
Hacer	
Desconectar	
Aumentar	
Usar	
Ahorrar	
Tener	

4. Circle the correct verb for each sentence

a. Nos han **vuelto/desconectado/ahorrado** de la realidad

b. Nos han **vuelto/permitido/reducido** adictos

c. Ha **afectado/causado/hecho** muchas distracciones

d. Me ha ayudado a **hacer/aumentar/simplificar** mi día a día

e. Ha **hecho/facilitado/afectado** el ciberacoso

f. He **tenido/tuve/hecho** un ordenador portátil

5. Translate into English

a. Ha ayudado a organizarme mejor

b. Ha afectado negativamente

c. Sin embargo lo malo es que

d. Nos ha hecho más perezosos

6. Sentence puzzle

a. Desde he internet usado pequeña *Since I was little I have used internet*

b. malo Sin facilitado embargo, lo de internet ciberacoso es que ha el
However, the bad thing about internet is that it has facilitated ciberbullying

c. ayudado Me productividad ha a aumentar mi *It has helped me to increase my productivity*

d. Nos desconectado ha de realidad la *It has disconnected us from the reality*

e. Siempre buscar tenido he un y me ha portátil ayudado a información
I have always had a laptop and it has helped me to search for information

Conversación entre amigos (Part 1)

Hace un año, Antonia dejó de utilizar las nuevas tecnologías por completo. Amador le hace algunas preguntas para averiguar los motivos de su decisión.

Amador: Hola Antonia. Dime, ¿por qué dejaste de usar las nuevas tecnologías por completo?

Antonia: Hola Amador. Al principio, pensé que las nuevas tecnologías sólo tenían ventajas. En general, estaba a favor de estos dispositivos electrónicos porque han simplificado y mejorado mi vida, mi manera de estudiar y de comunicarme.

Amador: Entonces, ¿qué pasó?

Antonia: Rápidamente me volví completamente adicta a los videojuegos y las redes sociales. Estaba constantemente con mi móvil. Ya no quería salir de mi casa. Desafortunadamente, prefería pasar tiempo a solas con mi teléfono en lugar de reunirme con mis amigos.

7. Find the Spanish for the following words in the conversation

a. (She) stopped

b. Questions

c. To find out

d. To use

e. Hi

f. At the beginning

g. I thought that

h. Advantages

i. Electronic devices

j. I study

k. Social media

l. Alone

m. To meet

8. Answer the questions in English

a. What did Antonia think about new technologies at the beginning?

b. What are the two areas of her life that electronic devices particularly changed at first?

-

-

c. Why did she stop using electronic devices?

d. How did new technologies affect her relationships?

9. Complete the translation from the second answer

I _____ very _____ completely _____ to video games and _____ _____. I was _____ on my _____ phone. I didn't want to ___ _____ of my _____ anymore. Unfortunately, I _____ to _____ time ___ ___ _____ on my phone instead of _____ my friends.

10. Circle the correct English translation

		1	2	3
a.	**Las ventajas**	*The vantage point*	*The advantages*	*The windows*
b.	**Han revolucionado**	*They revealed*	*They wasted*	*They revolutionized*
c.	**En lugar de**	*Instead of*	*In person*	*At the house of*
d.	**Me volví**	*I guessed*	*I am divine*	*I became*

11. Turn the following verbs in the present perfect tense and then translate into English

Present	Present perfect	English Translation
Pienso que		
Estoy		
Veo		
Son		
Me vuelvo		

12. Positive or Negative?

a. Estaba a favor de

b. Me he vuelto adicto

c. Sus ventajas

d. Ya no quería salir de mi casa

e. Desafortunadamente

f. Prefería pasar tiempo a solas con mi teléfono en lugar de reunirme con mis amigos

13. Quiz time: find the following items in the conversation above

a. A form of greeting

b. An equivalent for "han hecho más facil"

c. 2 question words

d. 3 adjectives

e. 5 verbs in the infinitive

f. 2 nouns

g. An equivalent for "quedar con mis amigos"

h. 4 verbs in the imperfect

14. Translate into English

a. Ha dejado de utilizar

b. Después de un año

c. Al principio

d. En lugar de

e. En mi casa

f. Dime

g. Ya no quería

h. Reunirme con mis amigos

i. Mi manera de estudiar

15. Gapped translation

a. Desde h_____ un ___ — *For a year now*

b. _____ para averiguar — *Questions to find out*

c. _____ has _____... — *Why have you stopped...*

d. ...de _____ las redes sociales — *...using social media*

e. E_____ a _____ — *I was in favour*

f. Mi _____ de _____ — *My way of studying*

g. ¿Qué _____? — *What happened?*

h. _____ de mi _____ — *To go out of my house*

i. _____ mi tablet — *To use my tablet*

j. _____ el tiempo — *To spend time*

k. Las _____ sociales — *Social media*

16. Translate into Spanish

a. My way of communicating

b. To leave the house

c. Electronic devices

d. Unfortunately

e. To use new technologies

f. I became addicted to my mobile phone

g. I preferred spending time at home

h. New technologies have disconnected us from reality

i. I have always loved my laptop because it's practical

j. Social media has caused many distractions

Conversación entre amigos (Part 2)

Amador: ¿Cuáles fueron los efectos de esta adicción en tu vida?

Antonia: Ya no podía concentrarme en nada más. Pasaba todo mi tiempo en Instagram y Facebook. No podía concentrarme en mi trabajo escolar y descuidé a mis amigos y parientes. Así que tuve que separarme de mi móvil. Desafortunadamente, muchas personas como yo se han vuelto adictas a las redes sociales y pasan la mayor parte de su tiempo en ellas.

Amador: Según tu experiencia personal, ¿cuáles han sido los aspectos más negativos de las nuevas tecnologías?

Antonia: Lo peor para mí fue perder a mi mejor amiga Sandra. La ignoré sin darme cuenta y ya no nos hablamos. También había discusiones constantes con mis padres porque yo siempre encontraba una excusa para no salir con ellos o ayudar en casa.

Amador: ¿Echas de menos las nuevas tecnologías hoy en día?

Antonia: Sí, de vez en cuando. Lo que más me gustaba era que me facilitaban la investigación y me permitían hacer las cosas más rápido. Siempre usaba mi ordenador para hacer mis tareas, ya que gracias a internet tenía acceso a mucha información muy rápido, lo que me ahorraba tiempo.

17. Find the Spanish for the following expressions in the conversation

a. *I could no longer focus on anything else*
Y_ n_ p_____ c_____ _n n____ m__

b. *I used to spend all my time on*
P_____ t_____ m_ t_____ e_

c. *I had to separate myself from my phone*
T_____ q__ s_____ d_ m_ m_____

d. *I neglected my friends*
D_____ a m__ a_____

e. *From your personal experience*
D_____ tú e_____ p_____

f. *The worst for me* L_ p_____ p____ m__

g. *It was* F__

h. *To lose my best friend*
P_____ a m_ m_____ a_____

i. *I ignored her without realising*
L_ i_____ s_ d_____ c_____

j. *We don't talk together anymore*
Y_ n_ n__ h_____

k. *What I liked the most*
L_ q__ m__ m_ g_____

18. Answer the questions in English

a. What negative effects did her addiction to her mobile phone have on her life? (4 details)

-

-

-

-

b. What is the worst thing that has happened to her as a result of being addicted to her phone?

c. Who did she constantly argue with at the time and why?

d. What does she miss now that she doesn't have internet access anymore?

19. Match

De vez en cuando	*I always used*
Hacer las cosas rápido	*Non-stop*
Siempre utilizaba	*What I liked the most*
Tenía acceso a	*My computer*
Sin parar	*To do things fast*
Lo que más me gustó	*Thanks to the internet*
Mi ordenador	*From time to time*
Hacer mis deberes	*I had access to*
Muy rápido	*To save time*
Ahorrar tiempo	*Very quickly*
Gracias a internet	*To do my homework*

THE LANGUAGE GYM

20. Complete choosing the appropriate missing words from the options below

Lo _____ para mí fue _____ a mi _____ amiga Sandra. La _____ sin _____

cuenta __ ya no nos _____. También _____ discusiones constantes con _____ padres porque

yo siempre _____ una excusa para no _____ con ellos o _____ en casa.

ignoré	hablamos	darme	mejor
encontraba	mis	peor	y
ayudar	perder	salir	había

21. Correct the spelling/grammar errors

a. Mi mehor amiga

b. No podilla concentrarme

c. Ya no nas hablamos

d. Hacer les coses múy rápido

e. Tenía acseso a mucha información

f. También había discusions constantes

g. Desafortunadamente muchos personas se han vuelto adictas

h. De vez en cuanto lo hecho de más

i. Lo perro para mi

j. Tuve que separarme de mi móbil

22. Tangled translation: into Spanish

a. Estos *devices* electrónicos han mejorado *my* vida

b. Siempre he *hated* los teléfonos *mobiles*

c. Desde hace *time* he *avoided* las *new* tecnologías

d. Me volví adicta *very quick* a mi *tablet*

e. Siempre me han *liked* los *computers*

f. Siempre *I have been* en contra de *the* redes *social*

g. Han *simplified* la vida

h. *Yesterday*, lo que me *liked,* fue jugar a los *games* en línea

i. Nos ha *allowed* mejor *mobility*

j. Ayer *I used* mi móvil para *to talk* con mi novia

23. Translate the following two short paragraphs into Spanish

a. Last year, unfortunately, I became completely addicted to new technologies and more particularly to social media. I was constantly on my mobile phone and I lost my best friend. There were also non-stop arguments with my parents. I had to totally stop using the internet.

b. At the beginning, I thought that new technologies only had advantages. What I liked the most was the access to a lot of information very quickly. It was practical and efficient, but I spent too much time on my mobile phone.

24. Answer the questions using the Sentence Builder and the conversations from this unit for support, then practice with a partner

a. Según tú, ¿cuál es la influencia positiva de las nuevas tecnologías en nuestra sociedad desde su nacimiento?

b. Dame ejemplos de cómo las nuevas tecnologías han mejorado tu vida.

c. Desde tu experiencia personal, ¿cuáles han sido los aspectos más negativos de las nuevas tecnologías?

d. ¿Cuánto tiempo pasaste ayer en las redes sociales?

e. ¿Qué hiciste?

f. ¿Cómo fue?

Key questions

Según tú, ¿cuál es la influencia positiva de las nuevas tecnologías sobre nuestra sociedad en los últimos años?	*According to you, what positive influence have new technologies had on our society in the last years?*
Desde tu experiencia personal, ¿cuáles han sido los aspectos más negativos de las nuevas tecnologías?	*In your experience, what have been the most negative aspects of new technologies?*
Dame ejemplos de cómo las nuevas tecnologías han mejorado tu vida cotidiana.	*Give some examples of how new technologies have improved your daily life?*
¿Al principio estabas a favor o en contra de las nuevas technologías? ¿Y ahora?	*Were you in favour or against new technologies at the beginning? And now?*
¿Crees que podrías vivir sin tu teléfono móvil?	*Do you think you could live without your mobile phone?*
¿Crees que usas demasiado tu ordenador portátil? Explica por qué sí / por qué no.	*Do you think you use your laptop too much? Explain why/why not.*

Unit 5. Music (present tense)

Casi todas las tardes *Almost every afternoon*	**me gusta ir a la tienda de música** *I like to go to the music store*	**con mis amigos** *with my friends*
El fin de semana *At the weekend*	**compongo música** *I compose music* **escribo letras** *I write lyrics* **escucho canciones** *I listen to songs* **voy a conciertos** *I go to concerts*	**con mis compañeros** *with my classmates* **con mi hermano/a** *with my brother/sister*
En mi tiempo libre *In my free time*		**con mi mejor amigo/a** *with my best friend*
Entre semana *During the week*	**toco** *I play* **la batería** *drums* **la flauta** **la guitarra** **el piano**	
Todos los viernes por la tarde *Every Friday evening*		**con mi novio/a** *with my boy/girlfriend*

Lo que me encanta *What I love* **Lo que me gusta** *What I like* **Lo que prefiero** *What I prefer* **Lo que más me gusta** *What I like the most*	**es** *is*	**el flamenco** **el pop** **el rock** **la música clásica**	**porque me parece** *because I find it*	**alegre** *cheerful* **divertido/a** *fun* **melódico/a** *melodic*
	es desahogarme escuchando mi música favorita *is to de-stress (while) listening to my favourite music*			**antes de acostarme** *before going to bed*
	es descubrir grupos nuevos en Spotify *is to discover new bands on spotify*			**cada sábado** *every Saturday*
	es ensayar con mi grupo *is to rehearse with my band*			**después del colegio** *after school*
	es relajarme escuchando hip hop *is to relax while listening to hip hop*			**por la tarde** *during the evening*

Lo que no me gusta *What I don't like* **Lo que no soporto** *What I can't stand* **Lo que más rabia me da** *What annoys me the most* **Lo que menos me gusta** *What I like the least*	**es** *is*	**el jazz** **el metal** **el rap** **la música clásica**	**porque me parece** *because I find it*	**aburrido/a** *boring* **fuerte** *loud* **violento/a** *violent*
	son las canciones con letras machistas *are songs with sexist lyrics*			
	son las canciones cursis *are cheesy songs*			
	son los artistas sin ningún valor musical destacable *are artists with no noticeable music talent*			
	son los grupos demasiado comerciales *are bands that are too commercial*			

1. Match

La mayor parte del tiempo	During the evening
Entre semana	What I can't stand
Lo que me encanta	Most of the time
Lo que no soporto	Before going to bed
Lo que menos me gusta	During the week
Lo que más me gusta	What I like the most
Casi todos los días	Every Sunday
Antes de acostarme	What I like the least
Por la tarde	Almost every day
Todos los domingos	What I love

2. Translate into English

a. Lo que me encanta es relajarme escuchando mi música favorita

b. Entre semana toco la guitarra con mis amigos

c. Comparto canciones en línea casi todos los días

d. Voy a conciertos casi todos los fines de semana

e. De vez en cuando escribo letras

f. Lo que no soporto son las canciones cursis

g. Lo que más rabia me da son las canciones con letras machistas

h. Me encanta el flamenco porque es melódico

3. Choose the correct translation

	1	2	3
Grupos nuevos	New groups	New friends	New bands
El flamenco	Flamenco music	A flamingo	A flaming torch
El sonido	The son	The sound	The tone
Las canciones cursis	Cool songs	Ringtones	Cheesy songs
Lo que más rabia me da	What annoys me the most	What I love the most	What I hate the most
Un éxito	An instrument	A melody	A hit
Compongo música	I put on music	I compose music	I write music
Las letras	The tunes	The lyrics	the sounds
Comparto	I share	I sell	I get

4. Gapped translation

a. T_ _ _ el piano — *I play the piano*

b. Comparto c_ _ _ _ _ _ _ _ — *I share songs*

c. V_ _ a conciertos — *I go to concerts*

d. Toco la g_ _ _ _ _ _ — *I play the guitar*

e. La mayoría del t_ _ _ _ _ — *Most of the time*

f. E_ _ _ _ _ _ las letras — *I write lyrics*

g. C_ _ _ _ _ _ _ música — *I compose music*

h. La música c_ _ _ _ _ _ — *Classical music*

i. Me gusta d_ _ _ _ _ _ _ _ _ — *I like to de-stress*

j. Lo que me da r_ _ _ _ — *What annoys me*

k. Lo que me e_ _ _ _ _ _ — *What I love*

l. E_ _ _ _ _ _ _ _ _ — *Listening*

m. M_ p_ _ _ _ _ — *I find it*

n. M_ _ v_ _ _ _ _ _ — *Very violent*

5. Sentence puzzle

a. soporto Lo porque no el complicado parece que demasiado jazz es me
What I can't stand is jazz because I find it too complicated

b. guitarra semana la toco el con mis piano amigos Entre y
During the week, I play the guitar and the piano with my friends

c. que Lo es hop relajarme hip prefiero escuchando
What I prefer is to relax while listening to hip hop

d. con trompeta de semana toco la padre que fines es Los mi músico
At the weekends, I play the trumpet with my father who is a musician

e. heavy no parece demasiado me es que metal me violento gusta porque Lo el
What I don't like is heavy metal because I find it too violent

f. desahogarme Lo música me es escuchando mi que favorita encanta
What I love is to de-stress while listening to my favourite music

6. Split sentences: form logical sentences then translate

1	2	English translation
Escribo letras y	en YouTube	
Toco	tienda de música	
Me gusta pasear mientras escucho	conciertos	
Comparto canciones	grupo	
Voy a la	compongo música	
Me gusta ensayar con mi	violento	
Yo también lo encuentro	hip hop	
Me encanta ir a	la batería	

7. Anagrams

a. *Lyrics*   telrsa

b. *Guitar*   itarurga

c. *I compose*   comngpoo

d. *Cheesy*   cuisrs

e. *To rehearse*   nseayar

f. *Drums*   raebtía

g. *Records*   idsosc

h. *Old*   jveio

i. *Songs*   nnccsione

j. *Bands*   porgus

8. Complete with the missing verbs

a. Los fines de semana _____ letras de canciones

b. Lo que me encanta es _____ con mi grupo

c. Entre semana me encanta _____ escuchando jazz

d. Todos los viernes por la tarde _____ a conciertos de rock

e. Lo que menos me _____ son los grupos comerciales

f. Lo que más me gusta es _____ las canciones cursis

g. Lo que no soporto son los grupos demasiado _____

h. Casi todas las tardes _____ canciones nuevas en TikTok

ensayar	desahogarme	escuchar	escribo
comerciales	gusta	comparto	voy

9. Spot and write the missing words: there are two omissions per sentence

a. En mi tiempo me encanta ir a tienda de música

b. Durante semana la guitarra

c. Todos viernes comparto canciones las redes sociales

d. Lo prefiero relajarme escuchando música clásica

e. Lo que más rabia me son los artistas sin ningún musical destacable

f. Casi todas tardes toco la guitarra mi grupo

g. Que menos me gusta son las canciones de reguetón con machistas

h. Lo que encanta es ir conciertos rock con mis amigos

---

10. Translate into Spanish (phrase level)

a. *In my free time* E_ m_ t_____ l_____

b. *What I love* L_ q_ m_ e_____

c. *What I like the least* L_ q__ m____ m_ g____

d. *With my classmates* C__ m__ c_____

e. *Every Saturday* T____ l_ s_____

f. *I like to de-stress* M_ g_____ d_____

g. *I like flamenco* M_ g_____ e__ f_____

h. *During the week* E_____ s _____

i. *Too commercial (pl)* D_____ c_____

j. *With my girlfriend* C__ m_ n_____

k. *Too violent* D_____ v_____

l. *New bands* G_____ n_____

m. *Sexist lyrics* L_____ m_____

n. *What I like* L_ q__ m_ g_____

o. *Before going to bed* A_____ d_ a_____

p. *Cheesy songs* L__ c_____ c_____

---

11. Translate into Spanish (sentence level)

a. During the week I play the guitar and the piano with my best friend

b. What I like the most is to relax while listening to my favourite songs

c. Every Friday evening I go to rock concerts with my girlfriend

d. What I can't stand is heavy metal because I find it too loud and violent

e. Nearly every afternoon I like to go to the music shop

f. What I like is to discover new bands on Spotify

g. Nearly every weekend I compose music and write lyrics

h. What I can't stand are bands that are too commercial

i. What I prefer is to rehearse with my band

j. What I cannot stand are artists with no noticeable musical talent

TEXT 1 – Lucas (16 años, Cádiz, La Laguna)

(1) ¡La música es mi pasión! Casi todas las tardes toco la guitarra y escribo letras con mi mejor amigo Andrés. Tenemos un grupo de pop y somos cuatro: un guitarrista, un bajista, un baterista y un cantante. Hacemos covers y también tenemos nuestros propios temas *[our own pieces of music]*.

(2) Lo que más disfruto es ensayar con mi grupo todos los sábados. Lo hacemos en mi garaje y, afortunadamente, mis vecinos son agradables y fanáticos del rock, ¡porque hacemos mucho ruido en el vecindario! Normalmente tocamos de dos a cinco horas, pero a veces el ensayo dura más.

(3) Los fines de semana, me gusta ir a la tienda de música, cerca de mi casa, para ver qué novedades hay en la música y descubrir grupos. De vez en cuando también voy a conciertos con mis amigos. Me encanta, porque siempre hay buen ambiente y me encanta escuchar música en directo. Sin embargo, lo que no soporto son algunas canciones de reguetón con letras muy machistas, como *Cuatro Babys* de Maluma.

(4) Durante la semana, a menudo comparto canciones con mi novia. Es genial, porque tenemos los mismos gustos musicales y además nos conocimos en un concierto de Maná en Valencia hace dos años. Maná es mi grupo favorito, me gusta mucho su estilo y me inspiran a componer mi propia música.

12. Find the Spanish equivalent in paragraphs 1 and 2

a. *Nearly:*   C

b. *Song lyrics:*   L

c. *A band:*   Un g

d. *A drummer:*   Un b

e. *A singer:*   Un C

f. *Bass player:*   Un b

g. *Pieces (of music):*   T

h. *What I enjoy the most:*   L

i. *To rehearse:*   E

j. *Noise:*   R

k. *In the neighbourhood:*   E e v

13. Complete the translation of paragraph 3

At the weekend, I like to go to the _____ _____ near _____ to see what _____ music there is and to _____ new _____. From time to time, I _____ go to concerts with my _____. I love it because there is always a good _____ and I love to listen to _____ music. _____, what I cannot stand are some reggaeton _____ with really _____ lyrics, like *Cuatro Babys* by _____.

14. These sentences were copied wrongly from the text above. Can you spot and correct the errors?

a. Me expiran a componer mi propia música.

b. Tenimos los mismos gustos musicales

c. Lo que no saporto

d. Mi encanta escuchar música en directo

e. Me gusta ver a la tienda de música

f. Casi todas las tardes toco la gitarra

g. Maná está mi grupo favorito

h. Porque hacemos mucho ruido del vecindario

i. De vez en vez también voy a conciertos

j. A mucho comparto canciones con mi novia

15. Translate the following phrases from Lucas's text

a. Lo que no soporto

b. Es mi grupo preferido

c. A menudo comparto canciones

d. Siempre hay buen ambiente

e. Qué novedades hay

f. Escribo letras con mi mejor amigo

g. Tenemos los mismos gustos musicales

h. Me inspiran a componer mi propia música

i. Hacemos mucho ruido

j. Nos conocimos en un concierto

TEXT 2 – Marina (15 años, Barbastro)

(1) La música es muy importante para mí. No pasa un día sin que escuche o ponga música. Es realmente parte de mi vida diaria y lo que me encanta es relajarme escuchando reggae en mi habitación después de volver de la universidad. Me gusta el reggae, porque es un tipo de música tranquilo y me resulta relajante.

(2) Entre semana, toco el piano todos los días. Toco el piano desde los cinco años y en el futuro me gustaría ser músico profesional, porque es mi pasión. Toco en un grupo de jazz y también en la orquesta de mi universidad. Lo que más me gusta, es ensayar con mi grupo los domingos. Tenemos nuestras propias canciones y tocamos regularmente para eventos locales.

(3) La mayor parte del tiempo escribo las letras y compongo las melodías de nuestras canciones. Me encanta, porque es creativo y emocionante en mi opinión. En mi grupo somos cinco: un violinista, un trompetista, un contrabajista *[double bass player]*, un baterista y luego yo toco el piano. También canto. Todos los viernes por la noche voy a conciertos con mis amigos. A veces viene también mi novio.

(4) Me gusta la mayoría de géneros musicales, pero por otro lado, lo que más me molesta son los grupos demasiado comerciales que están constantemente en la radio y los artistas sin ningún valor musical destacable. Prefiero grupos más independientes a los que realmente les apasiona la música, no solo el dinero.

16. Find the Spanish equivalent of the phrases below in Marina's text (paragraphs in brackets)

a. I play in a jazz band (2)

b. It is very important to me (1)

c. I write the lyrics (3)

d. Since I was five years old (2)

e. There is no day that goes by (1)

f. We have our own songs (2)

g. What I like the most (2)

h. Most of the time (3)

i. I would like to become (2)

j. There are five of us (3)

k. I like most musical genres (4)

17. True, False or Not Mentioned?

a. Marina plays many musical instruments

b. Her band doesn't create their own songs yet

c. There is a drummer in their band

d. She can't stand overly commercial groups with little noticeable musical talent

e. Her boyfriend writes their songs' lyrics

f. She prefers commercial bands

g. They have played a concert in a big stadium

h. She plays in her school's jazz band

i. She shares music videos on YouTube

18. Translate the following sentences taken from the text above into English

a. Me gusta la mayoría de los géneros musicales

b. En mi grupo somos cinco

c. A los que les apasiona la música

d. La mayor parte del tiempo

e. Tenemos nuestras propias canciones

f. En el futuro me gustaría ser músico

g. Que están constantemente en la radio

h. Los grupos demasiado comerciales

i. Me resulta relajante.

j. Lo que me encanta es relajarme escuchando reggae

k. Sin ningún valor musical destacable

l. Es realmente parte de mi vida diaria

19. Complete with the missing words choosing from the options provided below

El fin de semana me encanta ir a la _____ de música cerca de mi casa para ver las _____. De vez en cuando también voy a los _____ con mis amigos. Me encanta porque siempre hay un buen _____ y me gusta mucho la música en _____. Por lo contrario, no soporto a los _____ como Maluma que escriben canciones muy malas, en mi opinión, y con letras muy _____. Me gustan todos los _____ musicales. Otra cosa que me da un poco de _____ son los grupos múy comerciales que _____ constantemente en la radio. Toda la música suena casi igual.

novedades	tienda	directo	artistas	machistas
rabia	géneros	suenan	conciertos	ambiente

20. Select the correct sentence between the 2 below and explain why the other one is incorrect

1	2
Toco el piano desde los cinco años	Juego el piano desde los cinco años
Me gustaría estar músico profesional	Me gustaría ser músico profesional
Lo que me gusta es ensayar con mi grupo	La que me gusta es ensayar con mi grupo
Me gusta el reggae porque es un tipo de música tranquilo	Me gusta el reggae porque es un grupo de música tranquilo
Comparto canciones con mi novia	Comparto canciones con mia novia
Lo que mes me gusta, es tocar la guitarra	Lo que más me gusta es tocar la guitarra

21. Broken words

a. Las canciones cu_ _ _ _   *Cheesy songs*

b. los generos mus_ _ _ _ _ _   *Musical genres*

c. Un viol_ _ _ _ _ _   *A violin player*

d. Co_ _ _ _ _ _   *I share*

e. Lo que _e g_ _ _ _   *What I like*

f. E_ _ _ _ _ _ con…   *Rehearse with…*

g. …mi g_ _ _ _   *…my band*

h. Rela_ _ _ _ _   *Relaxing*

i. Una tie_ _ _ de m_ _ _ _ _   *A music shop*

j. T_ _ _ la trompeta   *I play the trumpet*

k. Un b_ _ _ _ _ _   *A bass player*

l. Me d_ rabia   *It annoys me*

m. Un g_ _ _ _ d_ jazz   *A jazz band*

22. Complete with an appropriate word

a. Me encanta porque siempre _____ buen ambiente

b. Nos _____ en un concierto de Maná

c. Me inspiran a _____ mi propia música

d. Es creativo y emocionante en mi _____

e. Me gusta la música clásica porque es _____

f. No me _____ el sonido de la trompeta

g. _____ gusta el flamenco porque es divertido

h. Me encanta _____ con mi grupo los domingos

i. Entre _____ me relajo escuchando jazz

j. Casi _____ las tardes toco el violín

k. Odio las canciones con _____ machistas

l. Compongo _____ y escribo letras

23. Translate into English

a. Toco la trompeta

b. Escribo letras de canciones

c. Lo que menos me gusta

d. Antes de acostarme

e. Todos los domingos

f. Me encanta ir

g. Lo que más me gusta

h. Lo que me da rabia

i. Por la tarde

j. Descubrir grupos nuevos

k. Escuchando reggae

l. Me gusta ensayar con mi grupo

m. Los grupos que son muy comerciales

n. Las canciones con letras machistas

o. Comparto las canciones

p. Lo que no soporto

24. Translate the paragraph below, using the chunks in the table on the right-hand side

I love music! I play the guitar and the piano very often. I also play the trumpet and the drums every day.

What I like the most is to listen to rock music in my bedroom. I also like to rehearse with my band. I write the lyrics of our songs.

During the week, I often share music videos and songs that I find on Spotify with my girlfriend. She loves music too.

Sam (15 años, Toledo)

También me gusta	todos los días.	la batería
Toco la guitarra	Escribo las letras	le encanta la música.
canciones que	la trompeta y	es escuchar música rock
en mi dormitorio	A ella también	Entre semana
encuentro en	¡Me encanta la musica!	Spotify con mi novia.
muy a menudo.	a menudo comparto	con mi grupo.
También toco	ensayar	y el piano
de nuestras canciones.	Lo que más me gusta	vídeos musicales y

25. Translate into Spanish

a. Most of the time

b. What I prefer

c. I play the trumpet

d. I share songs

e. I go to concerts

f. I find it cheerful

g. Rock is fun

h. Before going to bed

i. I like to de-stress listening to my favourite music

j. What I love is to discover new bands

k. The bands which are too commercial

l. I love to relax while listening to classical music

m. What I like the most is to rehearse with my band

n. What I don't like is heavy metal

o. What I cannot stand are cheesy songs

p. What I love is to discover new bands on Spotify

26. Translate the following sentences into Spanish

a. I love music. It is part of my daily life, much more than social media and the internet.

b. After school, I love to relax listening to rock music or classical music. Every day, I also like discovering new bands on Spotify and sharing music videos with my friends on Facebook.

c. I also play the guitar, the piano, the saxophone and the drums. What I prefer is the guitar.

d. I have a band with my boyfriend and two classmates. We play rock music. My boyfriend composes the music and I write the lyrics of our songs. I love rehearsing with my band!

e. What I prefer is to de-stress listening to my favourite music. I love pop because I find it melodic and cheerful. Classical music is also very relaxing.

f. I often go to concerts, on my own or with my boyfriend. There is always a good atmosphere. What I don't like are artists with no noticeable talent. I find this very annoying!

27. Write a 140-word composition in which you include the following points

- What type of music you like listening to and why

- What type of music you dislike and why

- What you like to do related to music in your free time

- What instrument you play and who with (if you don't play an instrument, please make it up or say which instrument you would like to play and why)

- What concerts you like going to and who with

Key questions

¿Te gusta escuchar música? ¿Por qué?	*Do you like listening to music? Why?*
¿Cuál es tu tipo favorito de música?	*What is your favourite music genre?*
¿Prefieres escuchar música en casa o ir a los conciertos? ¿Por qué?	*Do you prefer listening to music at home or to go to concerts? Why?*
¿Tocas algún instrumento? Si es así, ¿cuál?	*Do you play an instrument? If yes, which one?*
¿La música es importante para ti? Explica.	*Is music important to you? Explain.*
¿Cuándo sueles escuchar música?	*When do you generally listen to music?*
¿Con quién te gusta compartir música y por qué?	*Who do you like sharing music with? Why?*
¿Qué tipo de música te gusta menos y por qué?	*What is the music genre you like the least and for what reason?*

Unit 5. Music (past tense)

Anteayer *The day before yesterday*	**compartí unas canciones** *I shared songs*	**con mis amigos/as** *with my friends*
Ayer por la tarde *Yesterday afternoon*	**escribí la letra de una canción** *I wrote song lyrics*	**con mis compañeros de clase** *with my classmates*
La semana pasada *Last week*	**fui a la tienda de discos** *I went to the music shop*	**con mi hermana** *with my sister*
El fin de semana pasado *Last weekend*	**fui a un concierto** *I went to a concert*	**con mi mejor amigo/a** *with my best friend*
El viernes pasado *Last Friday*	**toqué la guitarra** *I played the guitar*	**con mi novio/a** *with my boy/girlfriend*

Cuando era más joven *When I was younger*	**me gustaba** *I used to like*	**descubrir grupos nuevos en Spotify** *discovering new bands on spotify*	**antes de dormir** *before going to sleep*
		ensayar con el coro del colegio *rehearsing with my school choir*	**después del colegio** *after school*
		relajarme mientras escuchaba música rap *relaxing while listening to rap music*	**durante el día** *during the day*
		soñar despierto mientras escuchaba música *daydreaming while listening to music*	**todos los domingos** *every Sunday*

Me gustaba *I used to like* **Me encantaba** *I used to love* **Prefería** *I used to prefer* **No me gustaba** *I didn't like* **No podía soportar** *I couldn't stand*	**la música** *...music*	**clásica** **jazz** **metal** **rock** **con letras tristes** *with sad lyrics* **con un buen ritmo** *with a good rythm*	**porque me parecía** *because I found it*	**bastante** *quite* **demasiado** *too* **muy** *very*	**aburrida** **alegre** **melódica** **motivadora** **relajante** **violenta**
	cantar	**canciones**	**con**	**mi grupo** *my band*	
	tocar	**el piano / la guitarra**		**mis amigos**	

Me acuerdo de una vez que *I remember one time when*	**fui a un concierto de** *I went to a ... concert*	**Rosalía** **jazz**	**con**	**mi padre**	**y conocí al/a la artista** *and I met the artist* **y compré una camiseta del grupo** *and I bought a band shirt*

1. Phrase puzzle

a. pasada semana La	*Last week*
b. la Ayer por tarde	*Yesterday afternoon*
c. tienda a Fui la	*I went to the shop*
d. letra la Escribí	*I wrote some lyrics*
e. canciones Compartí	*I shared songs*
f. concierto a Fui un	*I went to a concert*
g. encantó Me	*What I loved*
h. que Lo preferí	*What I preferred*
i. odié Lo que	*What I hated*
j. gustó Lo me que no	*What I didn't like*

2. Complete

a. _____ de dormir	*Before going to sleep*
b. _____ del colegio	*After school*
c. Todos los _____	*Every Sunday*
d. _____ el día	*During the day*
e. _____ mi…	*With my...*
f. …_____ amigo	*…best friend*
g. Mis _____ de clase	*My classmates*
h. _____ con	*To rehearse with...*
i. mi _____	*…my band*
j. Me _____	*I used to like*

3. Turn the following verbs and expressions into the imperfect tense and then translate into English

Present	Imperfect tense	English Translation
Me gusta		
Prefiero		
Odio		
No me gusta		
No soporto		
Me encanta		
Me molesta		
No puedo soportar		

4. Likely or Unlikely?

a. Compartí la letra

b. Ensayé con mi perro

c. Toqué la guitarra

d. Escuché la radio

e. Fui a un concierto con mi gato

f. Bailé con el coro de mi colegio

g. Me gustaba tocar el piano

h. Después de dormir fui a la tienda

i. Fui con mi novia al ensayo

j. Bebí café antes de dormir

k. Fui a la tienda de pingüinos

l. Compuse música en mi casa

5. Circle the correct verb for each sentence

a. La semana pasada **toqué/fui/vi** a la tienda de discos

b. Ayer por la tarde escuché rock, **me gustó/fue/soporté** mucho

c. Anteayer **toqué/soñé/compartí** unas canciones en TikTok

d. Lo que menos **me encanta/me gustaba/odiaba** eran los grupos demasiado comerciales

e. El fin de semana pasado **toqué/ensayé/compartí** el piano en un bar

f. Nunca podía **odiar/soportar/gustar** la música jazz

6. Correct the spelling errors

a. Damasiedo comerciales

b. Mientras escuciaba música

c. Lo qui no me gastaba

d. Me parecia muy melodica

e. El fin de semana pesado

f. Compartirí unes canciones

Conversación entre amigos (Part 1)

Juan: ¡Hola Marta! Háblame sobre la última vez que fuiste a un concierto.

Marta: ¡Hola Juan! La última vez que fui a un concierto fue el viernes pasado. Fui a 'Morriña Fest' en A Coruña para celebrar el comienzo de verano.

Juan: ¿Cómo fue?

Marta: ¡Fue realmente genial! Había música por todas partes: en los bares, en las calles, en las salas de conciertos y en la plaza principal. Además, el tiempo era muy agradable y todo era gratis.

Juan: ¿Con quién fuiste?

Marta: Fui allí con mi mejor amiga Laura, mi prima Alejandra y mi novio.

Juan: ¿Qué grupo te gustó más y por qué?

Marta: Fue mi grupo favorito de rock, Maná. Son mexicanos y me encanta su música porque, además de melodías bonitas, escriben buenas letras que hablan de temas importantes.

7. Find the Spanish for the following words or expressions

a. Tell me about

b. The last time

c. I went

d. How was it?

e. There was

f. Everywhere

g. The streets

h. Shows

i. Free of charge

j. The weather was very good

k. My boyfriend

l. To celebrate

m. I love their music

n. They are Mexican

o. They write good lyrics

8. Answer the questions in English

a. Which season starts on the same day as 'Morriña Fest'?

b. How was it?

c. What was the weather like?

d. How much did they have to pay to get in?

e. Where were the bands playing? (4 details)

f. Who did Marta go with?

g. What was her favourite band?

h. What does she mention about that band? (3 details)

9. Complete the translation of Marta's second and third answers

It _____ really _____ ! There _____ music _____: in bars, on the _____, in the auditoriums and in the main _____ .

_____ , the weather was very _____ and everything was _____ !

It was my _____ rock band, Maná. They are Mexican and I love their music because, in addition to beautiful _____, they write good _____ that talk about important _____.

10. Sentence puzzle

a. última fui La concierto que a un vez — *The last time that I went to a concert*

b. hermano en Ayer tienda de estuve discos la con mi — *Yesterday, I was at the music shop with my brother*

c. tiempo gratis era era muy El y agradable todo — *The weather was very good and everything was free*

d. amiga allí mi y Fui mi prima mejor con — *I went there with my best friend and my cousin*

11. Translate into English

a. Había música por todas partes

b. El grupo tocó en la plaza principal

c. El que más me gustó fue el grupo de reguetón

d. Escriben buenas letras sobre temas importantes

e. Hizo un día soleado. ¡Fue genial!

f. Para celebrar el comienzo del verano

g. Compartí las canciones con mi mejor amigo

h. La semana pasada escribí la letra de una canción

i. No me gustó el grupo de música metal. Era demasiado fuerte.

j. Lo que más me gustó era escuchar hip hop mientras viajaba

k. El verano pasado fui a ensayar con mi grupo todos los viernes

l. Toqué la guitarra y también canté

12. Add the missing words or letters

a. Comienzo ____ verano

b. __ que ___ me molestó fue __ ruido

c. Fueron ____ grupos comerciales

d. __ viernes pasado fui a __ concierto

e. La m__ica con let__s trist__

f. __ música rock __ parece genial

g. Fui _ 'Morriña Fest' ___ mi prima

h. ___ celebrar el com___zo del verano

i. ___ la tarde ensayé ___ mi grupo

j. Mi g__po favo__to de __zz

k. El ___ de semana _____

l. La músi__ c__ un b__n ri__o

13. Categories: sort the items below into the right column

Mi prima	En un concierto	Anteayer	En La Coruña
En la calle	En la plaza	Interesante	En verano
Bien	Antes de	El mes pasado	Mi hermano
El sábado	Mis amigos	Genial	Violento

¿Quién?	¿Dónde?	¿Cuándo?	¿Cómo?

14. Positive or negative

a. ¡Fue realmente genial!

b. No me gustó nada

c. Lo que me encantaba

d. Lo que más me molestó

e. No pude soportar

f. Lo que odié

g. Lo que preferí

h. Demasiado violenta

i. Escriben buenas letras

j. Muy relajante

k. Conocí al artista

15. Match questions and answers

¿Adónde fuiste la semana pasada?	¡Fue realmente genial! Había música por todas partes
¿Cómo fue?	Volví a la una menos cuarto de la madrugada
¿Con quién fuiste?	El viernes pasado fui a un concierto de jazz
¿A qué hora volviste?	Fui con mi mejor amigo, mi prima y su novio

Conversación entre amigos (Part 2)

Juan: ¿Alguna vez has intentado aprender a tocar un instrumento musical? Si es así, ¿cuál?

Marta: Empecé a tocar el piano cuando tenía cinco años. Me gustaría ser músico profesional algún día. Siempre ha sido mi pasión y mi sueño también.

Juan: ¿Alguna vez has tocado en un grupo?

Marta: Sí, he tocado en tres grupos en total. Un grupo de rock, la orquesta de la universidad y ahora toco en un grupo de jazz.

Juan: ¿Alguna vez has tocado en público?

Marta: Sí. El mes pasado tocamos por primera vez en un festival de jazz. Lo que más me gustó fue el ambiente porque había mucha gente. Tocamos nuestras propias canciones y creo que el público disfrutó de nuestra música. Vendimos algunos discos al final del concierto, ¡lo cual es una buena señal!

Juan: ¿Quién escribe la música y las letras en tu grupo?

Marta: Depende. Todos aportamos algo. Anteayer escribí una nueva canción y también compuse la melodía enseguida. Me encantó tocar la canción por primera vez para mi novio y a él le gustó mucho, así que yo estaba feliz.

16. Answer the questions in English

a. How old was Marta when she started playing the piano?

b. What job would she like to do?

c. What's the word for "my dream" in the conversation?

d. What happened last month?

e. What did she like the most at the jazz festival and why?

f. How does she know the public liked their music?

g. Who writes the music and the lyrics in her band?

h. When did she write her latest song?

i. Who did she play the tune to for the first time?

j. What is the contrary of "al principio" in Spanish?

k. How would you translate the expression "enseguida" into English?

17. Split sentences

Vendimos algunos	melodía enseguida
Lo cual es una	una nueva canción
Empecé a tocar el piano	un grupo de jazz
Lo que más me gustó	así que estaba feliz
También compuse la	discos al final del concierto
Ahora toco en	tocar un instrumento?
Le gustó mucho,	buena señal
¿Has intentado	de nuestra música
El público disfrutó	fue el ambiente
Anteayer escribí	cuando tenía cinco años

18. Translate into Spanish

a. It depends

b. I wrote a new song

c. We played for the first time

d. There were a lot of people

e. Have you ever played in public?

f. At the end of the concert

g. What I liked the most was the atmosphere

h. It has always been my dream

i. I started to play the piano

j. I also composed the melody straight away

k. I have had three bands in total

19. Complete the following sentences with appropriate words

a. Escribo letras de _____

b. Compré una _____ del grupo

c. El viernes pasado _____ con mi banda

d. Me gustó el _____ porque había mucha gente

e. Antes de dormir _____ música en Spotify

f. Me molesta la música metal porque es _____

g. Lo que me encantó fue el _____ de flamenco

h. Tocamos por _____ vez en un festival de jazz

i. _____ una nueva canción y compuse la melodía

j. Lo mejor fue cuando _____ al artista

20. Tangled translation: into Spanish

a. Vendimos *some* discos al final del *concert*

b. Me encantó *play* la canción *for* primera *time* para mi *boyfriend*

c. ¿Alguna vez *you have* tocado *in* público?

d. Me gustaría *become* en *musician* profesional.

e. *I started* a tocar el piano *when* tenía *five* años

f. Lo que más me *liked* fue el *atmosphere*

g. ¡Lo *which* es una buena *sign*!

h. Creo *that* el público *enjoyed* de *our* música

i. Sí, he *had* tres *bands* en total. *One* grupo de rock, la orquesta de la *university* y *now* toco en un grupo de jazz.

21. Translate the following paragraphs into Spanish

The last time I went to a concert was last Saturday. I went to town with my best friend and my sister and we listened to a rock band at the local auditorium. It was great! What I liked the most was the atmosphere because there were a lot of people. After the concert, I bought a tee shirt and a record.

Last weekend, what I preferred was to rehearse with my band. We played our own songs. Recently, I wrote some lyrics and new melodies and we tried them for the first time. It was exciting!

I started playing the guitar when I was five and I had my first band when I was twelve. Now, I play for the school orchestra and also in a rock band. I have always liked playing music and I would like to become a professional musician one day.

Last week I went to the music shop near my house with my friends. I discovered some new bands and I bought two records. Later, I played the piano at home and then I listened to music on Spotify before going to sleep.

Yesterday, what I liked the most was to daydream while listening to hip hop after doing my homework. In the evening, I shared some songs with my best friend before going to sleep.

22. Correct the spelling errors

a. Me gusto relajarme escuchando musica

b. Alginos grupos fueron demesiado comertiales

c. Compre una camisseta del groupo

d. Escribé le letra de un canción y compusé lo música

e. Mi pareció demasiado violetna

f. Abía música por totoes partes

g. Buonas letras que hablan de temas importaint

23. Answer the following questions to the best of your ability using the Sentence Builder from this unit and the conversation above for support. Then practice with a partner

a. ¿Cuéntame sobre la última vez que fuiste a un concierto? ¿Cómo era? ¿Con quién fuiste?

b. ¿Qué música escuchaste en casa anoche? ¿Cómo era?

c. ¿Alguna vez has intentado tocar un instrumento musical? Si es así, ¿cuál?

d. ¿Alguna vez has tocado en un grupo? Si es así, ¿qué tipo de música?

e. ¿Qué grupo te gustó más este año y por qué?

Key questions

¿Cuéntame sobre la última vez que fuiste a un concierto? ¿Cómo era? ¿Con quién fuiste?	*Tell me about the last time you went to a concert? How was it? Who did you go with?*
¿Cuál era tu tipo de música favorita cuando eras más joven?	*What was your favourite music genre when you were younger?*
¿Qué música escuchaste en casa anoche?	*What music did you listen to at home yesterday evening?*
¿Alguna vez has tocado en un grupo? Si es así, ¿cómo fue?	*Have you ever played in a band? If yes, how was it?*
¿Cuándo fue la última vez que compraste música?	*When was the last time you bought some music?*
¿Con quién escuchaste música el fin de semana pasado? ¿Dónde fue?	*Who did you listen to music with last weekend? Where was it?*
¿Qué grupo te gustó más este año y por qué?	*What is the band you have liked the most this year and for what reason?*

Unit 6. Cinema and television (present tense)

Generalmente *Generally* Normalmente *Usually* Por lo general *In general*	(yo) nunca veo	*I never watch*	comedias	*comedies*
	(nosotros) ya no vemos	*we don't watch anymore*	películas	*films*
	ella no ve	*she doesn't watch*	series	*series*
	él solamente ve	*he only watches*	telenovelas	*soap operas*

Mi programa favorito *My favourite programme*	lo/la ponen una vez a la semana *is on once a week*	a las cinco (en punto) *at five o'clock (on the dot)*
Mi serie favorita *My favourite series*	lo/la ponen todas las tardes *is on every afternoon*	a las tres y cuarto *at quarter past three*
El concurso que más me gusta *The game show that I like the most*	lo/la ponen todas las noches *is on every evening*	a las ocho y media *at half past eight*

Me encanta ver *I love watching*	documentales *documentaries*	porque en mi opinión son *because in my opinion they are*	educativos/as *educational*
Me gusta mucho ver *I like a lot watching*	películas de acción *action films*	porque pienso que son *because I think they are*	interesantes *interesting*
Prefiero ver *I prefer watching*	películas clásicas *classic films*	porque los/las encuentro *because I find them*	emocionantes *exciting* fascinantes *fascinating*

Evito ver *I avoid watching*	los anuncios *adverts*	porque son *because they are*	aburridos/as *boring*
No me gustan nada *I don't like at all*	las películas románticas *romantic films*	porque me parecen *because I find them*	estúpidos/as *stupid*
Odio sobre todo *I hate above all*	los *reality show* *reality shows*		una pérdida de tiempo *a waste of time*

Nunca me pierdo *I never miss*	un episodio *an episode*	de mi serie favorita *of my favourite series*
		de mi programa favorito *of my favourite TV show*

En mi opinión *In my opinion* Creo que *I believe that* A mi parecer *According to me*	los concursos *TV contests* los dibujos animados *cartoons* los documentales *documentaries* las películas *films* las telenovelas *soap operas*	son *are*	tan *as* menos *less* más *more*	graciosos/as *comical* entretenidos/as *entertaining* dramáticos/as *dramatic* divertidos/as *funny*	como *as* que *than*	los programas deportivos *sports programmes* las noticias *the news* los telediarios *the news bulletin* las series de televisión *TV series*

1. Choose the correct translation

	1	2	3
Las telenovelas	TV contests	Films	Soap operas
Los concursos	The news	TV contests	Cartoons
Las películas clásicas	Classic films	New films	Horror films
Divertidísimo	Super fun	Super boring	Super interesting
Aburrido	Boring	Exciting	Stupid
Evito	I like	I believe	I avoid
Una pérdida de tiempo	A great time	A waste of time	Bad weather
Documentales	Adverts	The programmes	Documentaries
Noticias	The news	Cartoons	Series
Nunca me pierdo	I never watch	I never miss	I never like

2. Match

Generalmente	Exciting
Los dibujos animados	I think that
Emocionante	Episode
Lo ponen	I watch series
Los anuncios	In my opinion
Creo que	Fascinating
Estúpidos	I avoid watching
El episodio	Generally
Veo las series	Stupid
Evito ver	It is on
Fascinante	Cartoons
En mi opinión	Adverts

3. Complete with the correct option from the ones provided below

a. Mi _____ favorita la ponen todas las tardes

b. Prefiero ver las _____ de acción

c. Creo que las telenovelas son muy _____

d. Nunca me _____ un episodio de mi programa favorito

e. Odio sobre _____ los *reality shows*

f. El _____ que más me gusta lo ponen una vez al día

g. Por lo general ella no ___ comedias

h. En mi opinión los anuncios son tontos y _____

ve	todo	serie	concurso
películas	**pierdo**	**aburridos**	**graciosas**

4. Translate into English

a. Odio sobre todo los anuncios

b. Mi programa favorito

c. Es una pérdida de tiempo

d. Lo ponen todas las noches a las once

e. Evito ver las noticias

f. Las telenovelas son dramáticas

g. Creo que es entretenido

h. Ya no vemos las series de acción

i. Nunca me pierdo una buena comedia

j. Por lo general nunca veo los concursos

k. Esa serie es muy aburrida

l. En mi opinión, los documentales son educativos

5. Sentence puzzle

a. noches Mi ponen la media todas a las las ocho y favorita serie
   My favourite series is on every night at eight thirty

b. porque románticas ver parecen películas Evito aburridas me
   I avoid watching romantic movies because I find them boring

c. porque todo *reality* tiempo Odio sobre son *shows* una pérdida de los
   I hate above all reality shows because they are a waste of time

d. son opinión, animados mi los dibujos mucho entretenidos que las En más comedias
   In my opinion cartoons are much funnier than comedies

e. tardes El que ponen cinco gusta lo todas las a me las concurso
   The TV contest I like the most is on every afternoon at five

f. ver porque películas me fascinantes antiguas las Prefiero parecen
   I prefer watching old movies because I find them gripping

g. más mi Hollywood las yo, los son interesantes A parecer que películas de documentales
   According to me, documentaries are more interesting than Hollywood movies

---

6. Spot and write in the missing word: one word is missing from each sentence

a. El concurso que más me gusta lo todas las tardes a las siete en punto

b. Me gusta mucho ver los documentales son interesantes y educativos

c. Nunca me pierdo mi deportivo favorito.

d. Ella todas las telenovelas que ponen en la tele

e. En mi opinión, las noticias son aburridas como los anuncios

f. Prefiero ver las series en Netflix que las en el cine porque son más emocionantes

g. Generalmente nunca veo comedias porque estúpidas

h. No me nada los *reality shows*

---

7. Anagrams

a. *Usually*   ormNmntalee

b. *Educational*   duEitvcao

c. *Adverts*   nAnusico

d. *Soap operas*   neTeoavells

e. *Exciting*   mooEcnaeint

f. *Documentaries*   oDusenmetcal

g. *Sport (adj)*   evtoprioD

h. *Never*   cuNna

i. *Fascinating*   acninesFat

8. Complete as appropriate

a. Mi telenovela _____ la ponen todas las mañanas

b. Evito ver las _____ románticas

c. _____ veo los anuncios porque me parecen estúpidos

d. En mi _____, los dibujos animados son tan graciosos como las comedias

e. Nunca me pierdo un _____ de mi serie favorita

f. Por lo _____ él solamente ve los programas deportivos

g. Prefiero ver los _____ sobre animales porque son educativos

h. Las películas románticas me parecen una _____ de tiempo

9. Complete the words

a. *Soap opera*   Tele_ _ _ _ _

b. *Programme*   Pr_ _ _ _ _

c. *Exciting*   Emoc_ _ _ _ _ _

d. *Usually*   Normal_ _ _ _

e. *Fun*   D_ _ _ _ _ _

f. *TV contest*   Con_ _ _ _ _

g. *Never*   N_ _ _ _

h. *Funny*   Gra_ _ _ _ _

i. *I avoid*   Ev_ _ _

j. *News*   Not_ _ _ _ _

10. Guided translation

a. *My favourite programme*   M_ _ p_ _ _ _ _ _ _ _ f_ _ _ _ _ _ _ _ _

b. *TV contests*   L_ _ _ _ c_ _ _ _ _ _ _ _ _ _ _ _

c. *In my opinion*   En m_ _ _ o_ _ _ _ _ _

d. *I don't like at all*   N_ m_ _ g_ _ _ _ n_ _ _ _

e. *Less boring*   M_ _ _ _ a_ _ _ _ _ _ _ _

f. *More educational*   M_ _ _ _ e_ _ _ _ _ _ _ _ _

g. *I never miss*   N_ _ _ _ _ m_ _ p_ _ _ _ _

h. *Because I find them*   P_ _ _ _ _ _ _ _ _ m_ _ p_ _ _ _ _ _ _ _

11. Tangled translation: into Spanish

a. Cuando *I have* tiempo libre *I spend* muchas *hours* delante de la tele

b. Odio los *reality shows because* son *stupid*

c. *My* serie favorita la ponen *all* los sábados a las *six* de la tarde

d. En mi opinión los *cartoons* son mucho más divertidos *than* las *news* y los anuncios

e. Mi padre *watches* los programas deportivos *all* las tardes porque le *loves* el fútbol

f. Mi *sister* ve muchas *soap operas* porque son *romantic*

g. *Never* me pierdo un *episode* de *my* documental favorito

12. Correct the spelling errors

a. Me purece   *I find it*

b. Una pérdada de tiempo *Waste of time*

c. El con curso   *The game show*

d. Emicionante   *Exciting*

e. Los dibujos ánimados *Cartoons*

f. Los annuncios   *Adverts*

g. A mi petecer   *According to me*

h. Invito ver   *I avoid watching*

13. Translate into Spanish

a. In my free time, I spend a lot of time in front of the television

b. I spend on average five hours a day watching cartoons, series and tv shows

c. My favourite TV show is on once a week every Thursday at five thirty

d. My favourite series is on every Friday evening, at quarter past nine

e. I also love watching action films, above all martial art movies because I find them exciting and funny

f. I almost always hate reality shows because they are repetitive and stupid

g. I never miss an episode of my favourite programmes

h. My father always watches the news

i. He says that the news are more entertaining than the cartoons and series that I watch

THE LANGUAGE GYM

TEXT 1 – Luis (15 años, Castellón)

(1) Por lo general, veo poco la televisión entre semana. Normalmente, nunca veo las telenovelas porque las encuentro aburridas y estúpidas. Por otra parte, me encanta ver documentales porque creo que son educativos e interesantes y además aprendo muchas cosas nuevas. También me encanta ver películas de acción porque son fascinantes y son mi género favorito.

(2) En cuanto a mi hermana gemela, ella solo ve series. Tiene una cuenta en Netflix y pasa la mayor parte de su tiempo libre delante de la tele. Pasa una media de tres horas al día viendo programas, películas y anuncios. Mis padres no están nada contentos y siempre le dicen que debería salir más a menudo de casa y leer más libros.

(3) Mi programa favorito lo ponen una vez a la semana, los sábados a las cinco. Se llama *Riding Zone* y se trata de un programa de deportes extremos como por ejemplo el surf, el skateboarding o el ciclismo de montaña. Me gusta mucho ver este programa porque siempre es entretenido y los deportistas que presenta son impresionantes.

(4) Lo que más odio son todos los *reality shows*. En mi opinión, este tipo de programas son una pérdida de tiempo, son ridículos y dan una versión falsa de la realidad. También evito ver las pelis románticas porque pienso que son aburridas. Sin embargo, lo que más rabia me da son los anuncios porque los ponen cada quince minutos. ¡Qué pesadilla!

14. Find the Spanish equivalent for the following in paragraphs 1, 2 and 3

a. *A bit*   U__ p____

b. *Soap operas*   L__ t_____

c. *I find it boring*   M__ p_____ a_____

d. *Exciting*   E_____

e. *I learn*   A_____

f. *A lot of new things*   M_____ c_____ n_____

g. *It is fascinating*   E__ f_____

h. *Only watches series*   S_____ v__ s_____

i. *Has an account*   T_____ u__ c_____

j. *More often*   M__ a m_____

k. *…of her free time*   d__ s__ t_____ l____

l. *are not happy at all*   n__ e_____ n____ c_____

m. *they put it on*   l__ p_____

n. *It is about*   S__ t_____ d__

o. *It is entertaining*   E__ e_____

15. Complete the translation of paragraph 4

What I _____ the most are _____ reality shows. In my opinion, these types of programs are a _____ of time, they are _____ and they give a false version of reality. I also avoid watching romantic _____, because I think they are _____. However, what annoys me the most are the _____ because they show them every _____ minutes. What a _____!

16. Answer the following questions about Luis's text

a. How often does he watch television during the week?

b. What programmes does he NEVER watch? Why?

c. Why does he enjoy watching documentaries?

d. Can you list four things Luis says about his sister in paragraph 2?

e. What is Louis's favourite programme? Why? What is it about?

f. What three reasons does Luis give for disliking reality TV programmes?

g. What other two things does he dislike about TV? Why? (Provide as many details as possible)

TEXT 2 – Carolina (19 años, Valladolid)

(1) Todos los sábados por la noche veo una película con mi familia. A veces es una película de acción y de vez en cuando es una comedia. Prefiero ver películas antiguas en blanco y negro porque me parecen más elegantes que las películas recientes. También me gusta ver dibujos animados con mi hermano pequeño. Son graciosos y divertidos, y mi hermano se ríe muchísimo.

(2) Mi seria favorita es *Alta Mar* y nunca me pierdo ni un episodio. Me parece divertida y me gusta mucho la actriz principal, porque es una mujer fuerte e independiente. También me gusta *La Casa de Papel* porque hay muchos actores españoles famosos, todos los personajes son muy diferentes y me gusta como trabajan en equipo para robar mucho dinero.

(3) En cuanto a mi hermano mayor, él nunca ve series. Prefiere ver documentales, sobre todo de animales o de naturaleza porque le parecen fascinantes. Su programa favorito es *Planet Earth*, le encanta porque es educativo y le apasiona el mundo natural. En el futuro quiere ser veterinario y por eso estudia biología en la universidad. En mi opinión, los documentales son menos divertidos que las series.

(4) Por lo general, evito ver los *reality shows*. Me parecen estúpidos y aburridos. Lo que también odio son los anuncios cada quince minutos durante una película. ¡Qué pesadilla! Además siempre los ponen en los momentos más interesantes de la película y cortan la acción y el suspense de la historia. Es un fastidio. Afortunadamente, en el cine no hay publicidad durante las películas.

17. Complete the sentences below based on Carolina's text

a. Every _____ night she watches a movie with her family.

b. _____ it is an action movie, and _____ _____ to _____ it is a comedy.

c. I prefer to watch _____ in _____ because I _____.

d. Also, I like to watch _____ with my brother because he_____ a lot.

e. My favourite series is *Alta Mar* and I never _____. I find it _____ and I really like the main actress because she is a _____ woman.

f. I also enjoy *La Casa de Papel* because _____ _____ actors.

g. My older brother never _____.

h. He prefers documentaries on animals because _____.

i. He has a passion for the _____.

j. Usually, I avoid watching _____ because I _____ them_____ and _____.

k. What I also hate are _____ every _____ during movies. What a _____!

18. Find in Carolina's text the Spanish equivalent for the following

a. From time to time

b. Old

c. In black and white

d. He laughs a lot

e. I never miss

f. Entertaining

g. Many

h. Famous

i. With regard to my brother

j. He finds them fascinating

k. His favourite programme

l. The natural world

m. Less fun

n. What a nightmare!

19. Fill in the gap using the options provided below

Todos los sábados por la noche, _____ una película con mi familia. A veces es una película de acción y de _____ en cuando es una comedia. Prefiero ver películas _____ en blanco y negro, porque las encuentro más elegantes que las películas recientes. También me gusta ver _____ animados con mi _____ pequeño. Son _____ y divertidos y mi hermano se ríe muchísimo.

Mi serie favorita es *Alta Mar* y nunca me _____ ni un episodio. La encuentro _____ y me gusta mucho la _____ principal porque es una mujer _____ e independiente. También me gusta *La Casa de Papel* porque hay muchos actores españoles _____. Todos los personajes son muy diferentes y me gusta como trabajan en equipo para robar mucho _____.

veo	hermano	conocidos	divertida	vez	graciosos
fuerte	dibujos	antiguas	actriz	dinero	pierdo

20. Translate into English

a. Es mi género favorito

b. Son educativos

c. No hay anuncios

d. Me parecen estúpidos

e. Los programas deportivos

f. En blanco y negro

g. ¡Qué pesadilla!

h. Él nunca ve series

i. Mi hermano se ríe muchísimo

j. Más elegantes que las películas recientes

k. Le apasiona el mundo natural

l. Durante la semana

m. Tiene una cuenta en Netflix

n. En mi opinión son aburridos

21. Combine the chunks in each column to make logical sentences, then translate them into English

1	2	English translation
Mi serie	no hay publicidad	
Me encanta ver	opinión son fascinantes	
Evito ver los reality	pérdida de tiempo	
¡Qué	shows	
En el cine	general ella ve solo comedias	
En mi	lo ponen todos los viernes	
Las noticias no son una	películas antiguas	
Nunca me	animados son graciosos	
Por lo	pierdo un episodio	
Mi programa favorito	pesadilla!	
Creo que los dibujos	favorita	

22. Tiled translation: translate the text below using the chunks of language provided in the table

During the week, I watch television every day. I spend about 2-3 hours a day watching movies or series on Netflix.

My favourite programmes are TV contests, cartoons and series. The programme I like the most is called 'Umbrella Academy'. I love fantasy series because they are exciting and full of action.

What I can't stand are TV reality shows because they are stupid and fake. I also hate commercials because they cut the action at the most interesting moments of a programme. What a nightmare!

interesantes de un	porque son estúpidos	porque cortan	Paso unas 2-3
El programa	animados y las series.	porque son emocionantes	¡Qué pesadilla!
de fantasía,	Durante la semana	Mis programas favoritos son	los *reality shows*
viendo películas	todos los días.	son	gusta se llama
Lo que no soporto	También odio	programa.	los dibujos
horas al día	la acción en	los concursos,	Me encantan las series
y falsos.	los momentos más	o series en Netflix.	veo la tele
'Umbrella Academy'.	y están llenas de acción.	los anuncios	que más me

23. Translate into Spanish (word level)

a. *A programme* Un p_____

b. *A series* Una s_____

c. *Interesting* I_____

d. *Commercials* Los a_____

e. *A documentary* Un d_____

f. *Favourite* F_____

g. *A TV contest* Un c_____

h. *A soap opera* Una t_____

i. *To watch* V_____

j. *In general* P___ l__ g_____

k. *During* D_____

l. *Fascinating* F_____

m. *Exciting* E_____

n. *News* Las n_____

o. *Nightmare* U__ p_____

24. Complete

a. Me encanta e_____ música

b. Prefiero ver d_____

c. Evito ver los a_____. ¡Qué p_____!

d. Nunca me p_____ un episodio de mi programa favorito

e. En m__ opinión los dibujos a_____son tan divertidos como las películas de a_____

f. La serie 'Wednesday' la p_____ una vez a la semana

g. Lo que más me m_____ son los anuncios. Los ponen cada quince m_____ en todos los canales de la tele

h. A mi hermana mayor le e_____ las c_____

i. C_____ que las películas antiguas son más e_____que las películas recientes

j. Por lo general él solamente ve los programas d_____, pero a veces le gusta ver los d_____ de naturaleza

k. El c_____que más me gusta lo ponen t_____ las tardes a las siete en p_____

25. Translate into Spanish (phrase level)

a. Luckily

b. What I can't stand

c. During the week

d. Every day

e. I spend

f. I hate above all

g. I find that

h. Sports programmes

i. Negative things

j. On the natural world

k. Exciting and entertaining

l. I learn

m. At the best moments

n. When there is

o. What a nightmare!

p. The programme I like

q. A series on Netflix

r. I avoid watching

---

26. Translate into Spanish (sentence level)

a. During the week, I watch television every day

b. I spend about three hours a day watching films, documentaries and series

c. I prefer action movies, documentaries on the natural world and police series. I find them exciting and entertaining

d. What I like about documentaries is that I learn a lot

e. What I can't stand is sports programmes, as I find them boring

f. I avoid watching the news because I always learn negative things about the world

g. What I hate the most, however, is commercials because they interrupt action at the best moments

---

27. Write a 140-word composition including the following points

- To what extent you enjoy watching television and why.
- How much time you spend watching television.
- What you watch normally and why.
- What your favourite tv programme is and how often is it on.
- What you dislike the most and why.
- What you think of tv-reality shows, commercials, Netflix series, sports programmes and the news.

28. Write a 200-word composition including the following points

- What the rest of your family enjoys watching (write a bit for each family member).
- What you did yesterday during your free time, including what you watched (on TV, social media, etc.) and how you liked it.
- What kind of movie you would like to watch over the next few days or weeks and why.
- What you plan to do tomorrow in your free time. Note, you must include, amongst other things (a) watching TV programmes and movies, (b) listening to music and (c) use of the internet.
- Say what programmes you used to watch as a child and what your favourite one was.

Key questions

¿Qué te gusta ver normalmente en la televisión? ¿Por qué?	*What you usually like watching on TV? Why?*
¿Cuál es tu programa de televisión favorito? ¿Cuándo lo ponen?	*What is your favourite TV program? When is it on?*
¿Prefieres ver películas o series? ¿Por qué?	*Do you prefer watching films or series? Why?*
¿Qué tipo de programa de televisión no te gusta? ¿Por qué?	*What is the type of TV program you don't like? Why?*
¿La televisión es importante para ti? Explica.	*Is television important to you? Explain.*
¿Cuándo sueles ver la televisión?	*When do you normally watch TV?*
¿Dónde te gusta ver la televisión? ¿Por qué?	*Where do you like watching TV? Why?*
¿Con quién te gusta ver la televisión? ¿Por qué?	*Who do you like watching TV with? Why?*
¿Cuánto tiempo a la semana pasas viendo la televisión?	*How much time do you spend on average watching TV each week?*

Unit 6. Talking about a movie (past tense)

Anteayer *The day before yesterday*	**compré una entrada para ver** *I bought a cinema ticket to see*	**una comedia** *a comedy*
Ayer por la tarde *Yesterday afternoon*	**fui al cine para ver** *I went to the cinema to see*	**un cortometraje** *a short film*
La semana pasada *Last week*	**fui a ver** *I went to see*	**una película de aventuras** *an adventure film*
El fin de semana pasado *Last weekend*	**fui con mi hermano a ver** *I went with my brother to watch*	**una película de miedo** *a horror film*
El viernes pasado *Last Friday*	**vi** *I watched*	**una película romántica** *a romantic film*

La película hablaba de *The film talked about*	**la historia de un superhéroe** *the story of a superhero*	**que tenía la misión de salvar el mundo** *who had the mission to save the world*
Trataba de *It was about*	**la vida de un personaje** *the life of a character*	**que estaba buscando a su alma gemela** *who was looking for his/her soulmate*

El tema principal *The main theme*	**era** *was*	**la amistad**	*friendship*
		la avaricia	*greed*
		la guerra (de Vietnam)	*the (Vietnam) war*
		la infancia	*childhood*
		la venganza	*revenge*
		el espionaje	*spying*
		el fin del mundo	*the end of the world*
		una historia basada en hechos reales	*a true story*
		una lucha entre el bien y el mal	*a fight between good and evil*
		un secuestro	*a hostage taking*

Me gustó mucho *I liked a lot* **Me encantó especialmente** *I particularly loved*	**la banda sonora** *the soundtrack* **la historia** *the story* **la puesta en escena** *the directing*	**porque era** *because it was*	**cautivador/a** *captivating* **cómico/a** *comical* **conmovedor/a** *moving* **graciosísimo/a** *hilarious*
No me gustó *I didn't like* **Me decepcionó** *I was disappointed with*	**el comienzo** *the beginning* **el final** *the ending* **la actriz principal** *the main actress*		**angustioso/a** *nerve-racking* **decepcionante** *disappointing* **mediocre** *mediocre* **previsible** *predictable*

Me gustaron muchísimo *I really liked* **Me encantaron** *I enjoyed*	**las actuaciones** *the acting* **las escenas de combate** *combat scenes* **los diálogos** *the dialogues* **los efectos especiales** *the special effects*	**porque eran** *because they were*	**fascinantes** *fascinating* **impresionantes** *impressive* **increíbles** *superb* **originales** *original*

1. Match

Un cortometraje	The acting
La infancia	A spying
Una película romántica	A horror film
Previsible	A science fiction film
La banda sonora	Childhood
Un secuestro	The ending
Un personaje	A cartoon
El fin del mundo	A romantic film
Una película de miedo	A short film
El espionaje	A hostage taking
El final	The soundtrack
Las actuaciones	Predictable
Dibujos animados	A character
La ciencia ficción	The end of the world

2. Complete the words then translate them into English

a. Una com_ _ _ _

b. La ava_ _ _ _ _

c. La act_ _ _ princi_ _ _

d. Decep_ _ _ _ _ _ _

e. El comi_ _ _ _

f. Los diá_ _ _ _ _

g. Increí_ _ _

h. Me decep_ _ _ _ _

i. Una his_ _ _ _ _ basada en hec_ _ _ real_ _

j. Graciosí_ _ _ _

k. Conmov_ _ _ _ _

3. Phrase puzzle

a. mundo fin del el — *The end of the world*

b. Vietnam la de guerra — *The Vietnam war*

c. reales una en hechos basada historia — *A true story*

d. escenas las combate de — *The combat scenes*

e. alma su a gemela Buscando — *Looking for his soulmate*

f. de una aventuras película — *An adventure movie*

g. escena la en puesta — *Directing*

h. una mundo misión el salvar de — *A mission to save the world*

i. para cine ver al fui — *I went to the cinema to see*

4. Anagrams: unjumble and translate the words/phrases

a. ruGera

b. emrsiIpneotna

c. gVnenzaa

d. áloogisD

e. avCutdiaro

f. idoMcree

g. lE mtea rpicaipnl

h. malA laeegm

5. Translate into English

a. Compré una entrada para ver una película de miedo

b. Me encantaron los efectos especiales porque eran originales

c. Me gustó especialmente la banda sonora porque era cautivadora

d. Me decepcionó la puesta en escena porque era mediocre

e. Me gustaron mucho los diálogos porque eran graciosísimos

f. La película hablaba de la historia de un superhéroe

g. Vi una película de aventuras. Me encantó el final

h. El tema principal era una lucha entre el bien y el mal

i. El fin de semana pasado fui a ver una comedia pero era previsible

6. Complete

a. El fin ___ mundo

b. Buscando a _____ alma gemela

c. Fui __ ver

d. Las escenas ___ combate

e. La puesta ___ escena

f. Una película ___ miedo

g. La lucha _____ el bien __ el mal

h. Fui ___ cine para ver

i. Basada ___ hechos reales

THE LANGUAGE GYM

94

7. Gapped translation

a. Anteayer _____ una entrada — *The day before yesterday I bought a cinema ticket*

b. Ayer ____ una _____ de aventuras con mi hermano — *Yesterday I saw an action movie with my brother*

c. La película _____ de la historia de un _____ — *The film talked about the story of a superhero*

d. _____ de la vida de una reina — *It was about the life of a queen*

e. El _____ principal era la _____ — *The main theme was greed*

f. Me _____ muchísimo la _____ sonora — *I really liked the soundtrack*

g. También me encantaron los _____ — *I also loved the dialogues*

8. Complete the words

a. Una película rom_ _ _ _ _ _ — *A romantic movie*

b. Un_ película de m_ _ _ _ — *A horror movie*

c. El t_ _ _ princ_ _ _ _ — *The main theme*

d. Los efe_ _ _ _ especia_ _ _ — *Special effects*

e. La av_ _ _ _ _ _ — *Greed*

f. La in_ _ _ _ _ _ — *Childhood*

g. La gue_ _ _ — *War*

h. Las actu_ _ _ _ _ _ — *The acting*

i. La pues_ _ en esce_ _ — *The directing*

9. Break the flow

a. Megustaronlosefectosespeciales

b. Eltemaprincipaleraelfindelmundo

c. Lapelículahablabadelahistoriadeunsuperhéroe

d. Medecepciónólabandasonoraporqueeramediocre

e. Loquemásmegustasonlaspelículasdeaventuras

f. Tratabadelavidadeunpersonajequebuscabavenganza

g. Elviernespasadofuialcineparaverunacomedia

h. Unahistoriabasadaenhechosreales

i. Nomegustaronlasescenasdecomabteeranprevisibles

10. Gapped translation

a. Una película_____ — *A romantic movie*

b. El _____ principal — *The main theme*

c. _____ a su alma gemela — *Looking for a soulmate*

d. Los efectos _____ — *The special effects*

e. La _____ sonora — *The soundtrack*

f. La _____ en escena — *The directing*

g. La _____ de Vietnam — *Vietnam war*

h. _____ de — *It was about...*

i. La avaricia y el _____ — *Greed and money*

j. El fin ___ mundo — *The end of the world*

11. Complete with the missing accents

a. Los dialogos eran graciosisimos

b. Tenia la mision de salvar el mundo

c. La historia de un superheroe

d. Fui a ver una comedia y me encanto

e. La pelicula hablaba de la vida de una reina

f. Me decepciono el final porque era previsible

g. Compre una entrada para ver un cortometraje

h. Me gustaron muchisimo las actuaciones

i. La semana pasada vi una pelicula romantica

j. Me gusto la historia porque era comica

12. Sentence puzzle

a. agente vi de una película Ayer La hablaba de un acción. secreto. Película
Yesterday, I saw an action film. The film talked about a secret agent.

b. ciencia cine fui para ver al una de Anteayer ficción. Película
The day before yesterday, I went to the cinema. I saw a science fiction film.

c. actuación entre El era una lucha el y tema el. La era bien mala. principal mal
The main theme was the fight between good and evil. The acting was bad.

d. me me efectos gustó la sonora encantaron No los pero especiales. Banda
I didn't like the soundtrack, but I loved the special effects.

e. aburrida trama La y vi romántica. El era película pasado previsible. sábado una
Last Saturday, I saw a romantic film. The storyline was boring and predictable.

f. venganza tarde por una genial! la vi en cine. Trataba de Ayer ambición. ¡Era el dinero, película y
Yesterday evening, I saw a film at the cinema. It was about money, ambition and revenge. It was great!

13. Tangled translation: into Spanish

a. *Yesterday* vi una *film* de amor. ¡*It was* aburrida!

b. La película *talked* de la *story* de un *king* de Inglaterra y sus *eight* esposas.

c. Ayer *I watched* una *comedy* con *my* prima. ¡Nos encantó!

d. Me *disappointed* la *actress* principal. Era *mediocre.*

e. Trataba de la *childhood* de un *character* y su *revenge.*

f. Los *dialogues* eran *fascinating* y las *acting* conmovedoras.

g. El final era muy *predictable* y no me gustó para *nothing.*

h. El tema *main* era un *hostage taking* durante la *war* de Vietnam.

14. Translate into Spanish

a. Theme	j. Entertaining
b. Soundtrack	k. Disappointing
c. Money	l. Boring
d. Directing	m. Predictable
e. Acting	n. Good
f. Ending	o. Evil
g. The story	p. Greed
h. Exciting	q. Main
i. Nerve-racking	r. It was about

15. Guided translation

a. L_ p_ _ _ _ _ _ _ t_ _ _ _ _ d_ ...   *The movie was about...*

b. ...l_ l_ _ _ _ e_ _ _ _ e b_ _ _ y e_ m_ _   *...the fight between good and evil*

c. L_ b_ _ _ _ s_ _ _ _ _ e_ _ g_ _ _ _ _   *The soundtrack was superb*

d. E_ t_ _ _ p_ _ _ _ _ _ _ _ e_ _ l g_ _ _ _   *The main theme was war*

e. L_ _ e_ _ _ _ _ _ d_ c_ _ _ _ e_ _ f_ _ _ _ _ _ _ _ _   *The combat scenes were fascinating*

f. La h_ _ _ _ _ _ _ n_ e_ _ c_ _ _ _ _ _ _ _ _ _   *The story wasn't captivating*

g. A_ _ _ v_ u_ _ p_ _ _ _ _ _ r_ _ _ _ _ _ _   *Yesterday, I saw a romantic movie*

h. T_ _ _ _ _ d_ d_ _ _ _ y a_ _ _ _ _ _   *It was about money and greed*

i. L_ p_ _ _ _ _ _ h_ _ _ _ _ d_ f_ _ d_ _ m_ _ _ _   *The film talked about the end of the world*

Conversación entre amigos (Part 1)

Pregunta: Háblame sobre la última película que viste en el cine.

Lorena: Yo, el fin de semana pasado, compré una entrada de cine para ver una comedia. Se llamaba *Campeones* y los actores principales eran Javier Gutiérrez y Juan Margallo. La historia cuenta cómo Marco, un entrenador de baloncesto, tiene que entrenar a un nuevo equipo muy especial. Son un grupo de personas con discapacidad mental. Es una película conmovedora y reconfortante *[heartwarming]* en la que no faltan los momentos de risa *[that make you laugh]*.

Sonia: La última vez que fui al cine fue el sábado pasado y vi una película de Pedro Almodóvar *Madres Paralelas*. Me decepcionó mucho porque los diálogos parecían forzados y la actuación de los actores principales, Penélope Cruz e Israel Elejalde, fue muy mediocre. Sé que Penélope fue nominada a varios premios en el mundo del cine y ha ganado algunos de ellos, pero a mí no me gustó nada. Por otro lado me encantó Rossy de Palma, una de mis actrices españolas favoritas. ¡Como siempre, estuvo genial!

16. Find the Spanish for the following

a. *A cinema ticket*   U__ e_____ d_ c____

b. *It was called*   S_ l_____

c. *The history tells*   L_ h_____ c_____

d. *Coach*   E_____

e. *Basketball*   B_____

f. *Mental disability*   D_____ m_____

g. *Heartwarming*   R_____

h. *Hilarious moments*   M_____ d_ r_____

i. *The last time*   L_ u____ v__

j. *They seemed forced*   P_____ f_____

k. *She was nominated*   F__ n_____

l. *In the cinema world*   E_ e_ m_____ d__ c____

m. *Actresses*   A_____

n. *One of*   U__ d_ l__

o. *Favourites*   F_____

p. *As always*   C____ s_____

q. *On the other hand*   P__ o____ l__

r. *She was great*   E____ g_____

17. Complete the translation of Sonia's text

The last _____ I went to the _____ was last Saturday and I _____ a film by Pedro Almodóvar "Parallel Mothers". I was very _____ because the dialogues seemed _____ and the _____ of the main actors, Penelope Cruz and Israel Elejalde, was very _____. I know that Penelope was _____ for several _____ in the world of cinema and she has _____ some of them, but I didn't like it _____. On the other _____, I loved Rossy de Palma, one of my _____ Spanish actresses. She was great as _____!

18. Complete the text below with the options provided in the table

Jesús: La _____ película que vi en el cine fue_____. Fui a la sesión de las 14:00 con mi hermano y su _____ y vimos una película estadounidense de _____: *Top Gun Maverick*. En esa secuela de la película de 1986, Tom Cruise recupera su _____ estrella, el mejor piloto de la _____ del cine. Me encantaron las _____ de combate en el aire y los _____ especiales porque fueron realmente_____. Lo más increíble es que Tom Cruise no _____ ayuda de un doble de _____ porque ¡todas las acrobacias las hizo él mismo! A mi hermano le _____mucho la banda _____, pero a su amigo la película le pareció poco sorprendente y bastante_____. De todas _____, a mí no me decepcionó.

acción	necesitó	gustó	anteayer	efectos
historia	previsible	escenas	fascinantes	sonora
personaje	última	riesgo	formas	amigo

THE LANGUAGE GYM

97

Conversación entre amigos (Part 2)

Jesús: La última película que vi en el cine fue anteayer. Fui a la sesión de las 14:00 con mi hermano gemelo y vimos una película estadounidense de acción *Top Gun Maverick*. En esa secuela de la película del 1986 Tom Cruise resuscita *[revives]* su personaje estrella, el mejor piloto de la historia de cine. Me encantaron las escenas de combate en el aire y los efectos especiales porque fueron realmente fascinantes. Lo más increíble es que Tom Cruise no necesita ayuda de un doble de riesgo *[stuntman]* ¡porque todas las acrobacias las hace él mismo! A mi hermano le gustó mucho la banda sonora pero la película le pareció poco sorprendente y bastante previsible. De todas formas a mí no me decepcionó.

Ángel: La última vez que vi una película en la pantalla grande fue anoche. Fui al cine con mi novia y compré palomitas de maíz y bebidas antes de sentarnos. Vimos una película de dibujos animados que se llama *Coco*. La historia está basada en México y muestra celebraciones del Día de los Muertos contando una emotiva historia de una familia mexicana. El protagonista es un niño que lucha por cumplir sus sueños pese a *[despite]* todos los obstáculos. Me encantó todo de la película: la historia, la animación y la banda sonora.

19. True, False or Not mentioned?

a. Jesús went to the movies yesterday

b. He went with his girlfriend

c. They watched an American action film

d. In the movie, the main character was riding motorbikes

e. The movie was a sequel of an old film from the 80s

f. The cinema was full of people

g. Tom Cruise needed a stuntman to replace him in dangerous scenes

h. The special effects were really fascinating

i. Jesús' brother didn't like the soundtrack

20. Find the Spanish for the following in Jesús' text

a. Session

b. Twin brother

c. We watched

d. An American movie

e. The most incredible

f. A stuntman

g. The movie seemed to him

h. Acrobatics

i. The best pilot in cinema history

21. Answer the following questions about the two texts above

a. When did Jesús and Ángel last go to the cinema?

b. What type of movie did Jesús watch?

c. Is "Top Gun" a brand-new title?

d. What does the main character played by Tom Cruise do?

e. What does "un doble de riesgo" mean?

f. Who did Ángel go to the cinema with?

g. What was the movie he watched about?

h. What did he particularly like?

i. Where did the action take place?

j. What did Ángel buy before watching the movie?

THE LANGUAGE GYM

22. Complete with the options provided (from memory, without looking at the original text)

Ángel: La _____ vez que vi una película en la pantalla grande fue _____. Fui al cine con mi novia y _____ palomitas de maíz y bebidas antes de sentarnos. _____ una película de dibujos animados que se llama *Coco*. La _____ está basada en México y muestra _____ del Día de los Muertos, contando una emotiva _____ de una familia mexicana. El _____ es un niño que lucha por cumplir sus _____ pese a todos _____ obstáculos. Me encantó todo de _____ película: la historia, la animación y la banda _____.

se llama	los	última	celebraciones	la	sueños
compré	historia	vimos	protagonista	anoche	sonora

23. Split sentences join the two chunks in each column to make logical sentences then translate them

1	2	English translation
Compré un billete	fin del mundo	
El tema principal	vi una comedia	
Fui al cine a ver	muchísimo los diálogos	
Me decepcionó	para ver una película	
Me gustaron	de un secuestro	
Trataba	era la amistad	
El viernes pasado	la banda sonora	
La película habla del	una película de miedo	

24. Translate into English

a. La semana pasada

b. Un doble de riesgo

c. Anteayer

d. Mi novia

e. Compré palomitas de maíz

f. Antes de sentarnos

g. Una película de dibujos animados

h. La historia está basada en

i. Muestra celebraciones del Día de los Muertos

j. Lucha por cumplir sus sueños

k. Pese a los obstáculos

l. La última vez que vi una película

m. En la pantalla grande

n. Me encantó todo

o. Una familia mexicana

25. Complete

a. La _ _ _ _ ma película que vi

b. Me encan_ _ _ _ _ las escenas de combate

c. Una historia b_ _ _ _ _ en hechos reales

d. Las act_ _ _ _ _ _ _ _ eran mediocres

e. No me gustó n_ _ _ la historia

f. El tema prin_ _ _ _ _ era la guerra

g. Una l_ _ _ _ entre el bien y el mal

h. Compré p_ _ _ _ _ _ _ de maíz

i. Fui al cine con mi n_ _ _ _

j. Vimos una película esta_ _ _ _ _ _ _ _ _

k. Los di_ _ _ _ _ animados

l. Un chico buscando a su alma g_ _ _ _ _

26. Tiled translation: translate the text below using the chunks of language provided in the table

Two days ago I bought a cinema ticket to watch a spy movie. I went there with my girlfriend and her sister.

There were a lot of people because it was a Sunday. I liked the movie a lot because it was fun and the dialogues were hilarious. The directing and the acting were very good too and there were some really good special effects.

The movie was full of action and there were some exciting combat scenes. I would watch it again one more time.

Había mucha gente	La película estuvo	película porque	y su hermana.
La volvería a	entrada de cine para	y hubo algunas escenas	La dirección y las
fueron muy	compré una	de espías.	Me gustó mucho la
efectos especiales	con mi novia	buenas y	llena de acción
era divertida	ver una vez más.	hubo algunos	de combate apasionantes.
y los diálogos	Fui allí	porque era domingo.	realmente buenos.
actuaciones también	ver una película	eran graciosísimos.	Hace dos días

27. Gapped translation

a. La _____ hablaba de una _____ de amor — *The movie talked about a love story*

b. Los _____ eran terribles — *The actors were terrible*

c. _____ de una historia _____ en _____ reales — *It was about a real story*

d. El tema _____ era la _____ — *The main theme was friendship*

e. Compré _____ para _____ *Top Gun* — *I bought a ticket to watch "Top Gun"*

f. La puesta en _____ era _____ — *The directing was disappointing*

g. Me _____ la historia y la banda _____ — *I liked the story and the soundtrack*

h. La película _____ de… — *The film talked about…*

i. …un _____ que buscaba a su _____ gemela — *…a man who searched for his soulmate*

28. Complete creatively inserting as many words as you like. Ensure the sentences make sense.

a. _____ compré una entrada para ver _____

b. Fui con _____

c. Antes de sentarnos pedí _____ y _____

d. La película trataba de_____

e. El tema principal era _____

f. Me encantaron _____ y _____ porque eran _____

g. Me gustó _____ porque era _____

h. Me decepcionó_____ porque era _____

29. Guided translation

a. *The main theme* E_ t_____ p_____

b. *The acting* L___ a_____

c. *The directing* L_ p_____ e__ e_____

d. *The film talked about war* L_ p____ h_____ d_ l_ g_____

e. *I loved the movie* M_ e_____ l_ p_____

f. *I found it boring* M_ p_____ a_____

g. *It was a romantic movie* E_ u_ p_____ r_____

h. *It was about a true story* U_ h_____ b___ e_ h____ r____

i. *I liked the special effects* M_ g_____ l_ e____ e_____

30. Correct the spelling/grammar mistakes

a. Un pelicula de miedo (2)

b. La acris principalle (2)

c. La mission de salvar el mundo (1)

d. Ante ayer compre una entrada (2)

e. La fin del semana pasada (3)

f. Un historia emocionanta (2)

g. Ví un cortometrage (2)

h. Estabo buscando a su alma jirafa (2)

31. Translate the following paragraphs into Spanish

(1) Two days ago I went to the cinema to watch an American comedy. It was about the story of a young man who was looking for his soulmate. Therefore, the main theme was love and romantic relationships. The film took place in London, but the main character was an American man. The movie was quite interesting and entertaining. The dialogues were comical and the directing was impressive. What I liked the most was the acting and the soundtrack.

(2) Yesterday I went to the cinema with my girlfriend to see an action movie. It was about a superhero who had the mission to save the world. The movie was full of combat scenes and special effects. I loved that. I found that the movie was very entertaining with some comical scenes. However, the directing and the acting weren't always very convincing. Fortunately, the soundtrack was original and I loved the ending. My girlfriend didn't like the movie because she found that there was too much violence.

32. Translate the following paragraph into Spanish

My name is Javier. In my free time, I spend a lot of time on the internet, especially on social media. I know it is not healthy to spend too much time in front of a computer, but it is very entertaining. I usually spend three hours a day on Facebook, Instagram and TikTok. I also enjoy watching television. My favourite programmes are TV contests, police series and music programmes. I love music. In addition, I play the guitar and I love rehearsing with my band and writing lyrics of our songs. Finally, I love going to the cinema. Yesterday, I went to the cinema to see a science-fiction movie called *El Fin del Mundo*. It was about an alien invasion *[una invasión extraterreste]*. The action took place in New York. I loved it because the storyline was gripping and the combat scenes exciting. Moreover, the dialogues were often hilarious. The directing was very good too and I loved the special effects. I will definitely watch it again.

33. Write a 150 words composition including the following points

a. How you use the internet, especially social media and how much time you spend on them

b. The pros and cons of mobile phones

c. What you watch on television. What you like and what you dislike and what your favourite programme is and why

d. A description of a recent outing to the cinema saying:

- Who you went with

- What film you watched and what genre it was

- What it was about and what the main theme was

- How much you liked it; what you liked and disliked about it and why

Key questions

¿Qué viste en la televisión ayer? ¿Te gustó? ¿Por qué?	*What did watch on TV yesterday? Did you like it? Why?*
¿Cuál era tu programa de televisión favorito antes? ¿Cuándo fue?	*What was your favourite TV program before? When was it on?*
¿Qué fue lo que más te gustó ver en la televisión el fin de semana pasado? ¿Por qué?	*What did you prefer watching on TV last weekend? Why?*
¿Qué no te gustó ver en la televisión la semana pasada? ¿Por qué?	*What did you not like watching on television last week? Why?*
Cuando eras más joven, ¿la televisión era importante para ti? Explica.	*When you were younger, was television important to you? Explain.*
¿Cuándo fue la última vez que viste televisión? ¿Cómo era?	*When did you watch TV for the last time? How was it?*
¿Con quién viste la tele ayer por la tarde? ¿Dónde fue?	*Who did you watch TV with yesterday afternoon? Where was it?*
¿Viste alguna película buena en la televisión esta semana?	*Did you watch any good films on television this week?*
¿Cuánto tiempo pasaste viendo la televisión la semana pasada?	*How much time did you spend watching TV last week?*

Unit 7. Charity and voluntary work (present tense)

Ayudo en una asociación benéfica *I help in a charity*	**en mi ciudad** *in my town*	**cada semana** *each week*
Ayudo en una ONG *I help in an NGO*	**en mi instituto** *in my school*	**todos los domingos** *every Sunday*
Hago trabajo voluntario *I do volunteer work*	**en mi barrio** *in my neighbourhood*	**una vez al mes** *once a month*

Esto me gusta mucho *I like this a lot*	**porque me siento** *because I feel*	**útil** *useful*

Lo hago porque creo que	**es importante** *it is important to* **es imprescindible** *it is essential to* **es necesario** *it is necessary to*	**combatir** *fight* **luchar contra** *fight against* **reducir** *reduce*	**la pobreza** *poverty* **el paro** *unemployment* **las desigualdades** *inequalities*

Hay que *It is necessary to* **Debemos** *We must* **Se debe** *One must*	**ayudar a** *give assistance to* **apoyar a** *support* **echar una mano a** *give a hand to*	**los pobres** *the poor* **los más necesitados** *the most destitute* **los sin techo** *the homeless*

Es nuestro deber *It is our duty* **Es nuestra responsabilidad** *It is our responsibility*	**no ignorar** *not to ignore* **no olvidar** *not to forget*	**a las personas más necesitadas** *people in need* **a los desfavorecidos** *the underprivileged*

Para ayudar *In order to help*	**doy clases gratuitas de inglés** *I give free English lessons* **hago donaciones de comida/dinero/ropa** *I make money donations* **hago un voluntariado** *I volunteer* **sirvo comida** *I serve food*	**en organizaciones benéficas locales** *in local charitable organisations* **en un comedor social** *in a soup kitchen* **en una asociación caritativa** *in a charity*

Trabajo con	**indigentes** *the destitute* **refugiados** *refugees*	**desde hace dos años** *for two years* **desde hace cuatro años** *for four years*

A partir de ahora *From now on* **En el futuro** *In the future*	**me gustaría ayudar a** *I would like to help* **quisiera apoyar a** *I want to support*	**las personas mayores** *the elderly* **los niños discapacitados** *disabled childen*

1. Match

Asociación benéfica	To fight
Desfavorecido	A person in need
Un voluntario	Poverty
Olvidar	People
El futuro	Underprivileged
La pobreza	Homeless
El barrio	Charity
Combatir	Volunteer
Sin techo	To forget
La gente	Neighbourhood
Un necesitado	Future

2. Complete with the correct option

a. Ayudo en una _____ benéfica

b. Es nuestro _____ no olvidar a los desfavorecidos

c. Para ayudar hago _____ de ropa

d. Me _____ apoyar a las personas mayores

e. Hago trabajo _____ en mi ciudad dos veces al mes

f. Sirvo comida en un _____ social en mi barrio

g. Doy clases _____ de inglés para niños refugiados

h. _____ con refugiados desde hace dos años

deber	gustaría	trabajo	donaciones
voluntario	gratuitas	organización	comedor

3. Translate into English

a. Ayudo

b. Cada semana

c. Imprescindible

d. El paro

e. Las desigualdades

f. Útil

g. En mi instituto

h. Nuestra responsabilidad

i. Los niños discapacitados

j. Echar una mano

k. Luchar contra

l. Combatir la pobreza

m. Una ONG

n. Debemos apoyar

4. Broken words

a. Una asociación be_ _ _ _ _ _   *A charity*

b. Red_ _ _ _   *To lower*

c. Es nece_ _ _ _ _   *It is necessary to*

d. Un comedor so_ _ _ _   *A soup kitchen*

e. En el f_ _ _ _ _   *In the future*

f. Hago trabajo volun_ _ _ _ _   *I volunteer*

g. Las don _ _ _ _ _ _ _ de ropa *Clothes donations*

h. A partir de a_ _ _ _   *From now on*

i. D_ _ clases   *I give lessons*

j. Personas ma_ _ _ _ _   *The elderly*

k. Los sin te_ _ _   *Homeless*

5. The English translations below are wrong. Find the errors and correct them

a. En mi instituto	*In my town*
b. Los desfavorecidos	*Disabled people*
c. Trabajo con	*I think*
d. Las donaciones de comida	*Money donations*
e. Combatir	*Reduce*
f. Doy clases	*I help*
g. Quisiera apoyar	*I would like to appeal*
h. El paro	*Poverty*
i. Imprescindible	*Necessary*

6. Choose the correct option

a. Para ayudar **apoyo/doy/hago** clases de inglés en una **asociación/ONG/instituto** benéfica

b. Esto **mi/se/me gusta** mucho porque **se/me/le** siento útil

c. **Soy/Es/Está** nuestra responsabilidad ayudar a los **tan/menos/más** necesitados

d. Lo hago porque creo que es importante **luchar/combatir/ignorar** contra las desigualdades

e. A partir de ahora me **gustara/gustaría/gusta** ayudar dos veces **al/a/de** la semana a los niños más pobres en nuestro barrio

f. Es imprescindible reducir la **riqueza/pobreza/necesidad** y el **paro/bienestar/voluntariado** en nuestra ciudad

g. En el **presente/pasado/futuro** quisiera apoyar a las personas **viejas/mayores/antiguas**

h. Es **suya/tuya/nuestra** responsabilidad no **pensar/ignorar/omitir** a las familias sin techo

i. Trabajo con los **refugiados/recogidos/reprimidos** desde **hizo/hace/ha hecho** tres años

---

7. Find the Spanish for the following in activity 6 above

a. *It is necessary*   Es n_____

b. Most d*estitute*   L_ m___ n_____

c. *In the future*   En el f_____

d. *To give a hand*   E_____ u__ m_____

e. *Homeless*   L__ s__ t_____

f. *To support*   A_____

g. *I volunteer*   H___ t_____ v_____

h. *Poor*   P_____

i. *Refugees*   R_____

j. *To fight*   C_____

---

8. Match the words/phrases of similar meaning

Los sin techo	**Necesitado**
Enseño	**Viejo**
Asociación	**Luchar contra**
En el futuro	**Me gustaría**
Pobre	**Bajar**
Combatir	**Doy clases**
Reducir	**Olvidar**
Mayor	**A partir de ahora**
Ignorar	**Indigentes**
Quisiera	**Organización**

---

9. Sentence puzzle

a. combatir pobreza la Es imprescindible   *It is essential to fight poverty*

b. Cuando me ayudo siento útil a los demás   *When I help others, I feel useful*

c. sirvo comida ayudar en Para comedor un social   *To help, I serve food in a soup kitchen*

d. Me ayudar discapacitados a gustaría los niños   *I would like to help disabled children*

e. Hago en mi instituto voluntario trabajo   *I do volunteer work in my school*

f. asociación Ayudo benéfica en una   *I help in a charity*

g. apoyar Es necesario los más a necesitados   *It is necessary to support the most destitute*

h. ahora A de partir   *From now on*

i. gustaría trabajar mayores Me con personas las   *I would like to work with the elderly*

10. One of three

	1	2	3
Luchar contra	To play with	To fight against	To lean towards
En el future	In the past	Tomorrow	In the future
Soy voluntario/a	I am a volunteer	I am benevolent	I am a first aider
La gente pobre	Poor people	Rich people	Kind people
Los más necesitados	The luckiest	The bravest	The most destitute
Los niños descapacitados	Disabled children	Disabled people	Disabled adults
Las personas mayores	The youngsters	The elderly	The new generation
Apoyar	To bring food	To support	To give
Doy clases	I give money	I give clothes	I give lessons
Es necesario	It is necessary	It's your fault	It is faulty

11. Spot and write in the missing word

a. Ayudo una ONG

b. Hago un voluntariado en comedor social

c. En el futuro me gustaría ayudar los sin techo

d. Imprescindible reducir el paro

e. Trabajo los refugiados en mi ciudad

f. Doy clases gratuitas inglés a los niños pobres

g. Se debe echar mano a los más necesitados

h. Es importante luchar las desigualdades

i. Ayudo a los niños refugiados sus deberes

j. Hago donaciones ropa y dinero

12. Translate into Spanish

a. I give English lessons voluntarily

b. I help refugee kids with homework

c. I make money donations

d. It is necessary

e. In order to help

f. I serve food

g. I would like to support

h. It is essential to fight against poverty

i. I work with refugees and I like it a lot

j. I do volunteer work in my neighbourhood

13. Complete with a suitable word or phrase

a. _____ de ahora quisiera _____ trabajo voluntario en mi ciudad

b. Lo _____ porque _____ que es importante _____ contra las desigualdades

c. Para ayudar, dos _____ al mes _____ comida en un comedor _____ en mi barrio

d. Es _____ responsabilidad apoyar a los _____ necesitados

e. Me gusta _____ mi trabajo en la ONG _____ me siento útil

f. Ayudo en una _____ benéfica y _____ clases de música a niños discapacitados

g. En el futuro _____ hacer _____ de dinero a ____ organización local

h. Es nuestro deber no ignorar a _____ techo y echar una _____ para que encuentren un hogar

i. _____ los sábados voy _ una residencia en mi ciudad y ayudo a hacer la compra a las _____ mayores

TEXT 1 – Mateo (22 años, Elche)

(1) Ayudo en una asociación benéfica en mi ciudad todas las semanas. Estoy de guardia *[I am on duty]* todos los lunes y ayudo a los niños del colegio del barrio a hacer los deberes. Me gusta mucho hacer esto porque me siento útil y gracias a ello conozco a muchas personas interesantes y amables.

(2) Pienso que es importante luchar contra las desigualdades y todo el mundo debería poder tener la oportunidad de estudiar para poder tener éxito en la vida. Debemos apoyar a los más desfavorecidos y es nuestro deber colectivo no olvidar a los más necesitados, aquellos que no siempre tienen acceso a los productos de primera necesidad.

(3) Para ayudar, hago donaciones de dinero a organizaciones benéficas locales y sirvo comida en un comedor social de mi barrio una vez al mes. Es triste ver cuántas personas no se pueden permitir *[cannot afford]* pagar la comida. Desafortunadamente, el número de personas pobres ha aumentado a causa de la pandemia del coronavirus.

(4) Por otro lado, doy clases de español gratuitas a los refugiados desde hace dos años y creo que esta experiencia es muy enriquecedora *[rewarding]*. Hay personas de todas partes del mundo y es muy interesante para mí, ya que aprendo mucho de la cultura de sus países de origen. Lo que demuestra que, cuando das, siempre recibes algo a cambio.

14. Find the Spanish equivalent for the following in paragraphs 1 and 2

a. A charity	i. To fight against
b. Every week	j. Everyone
c. Homework	k. To succeed
d. Neighbourhood	l. In life
e. I feel useful	m. To support
f. I meet	n. The most underprivileged
g. Kind	o. Not to forget
h. I think	p. People in need

15. Complete the translation of paragraph 3 below

In order to _____, I make _____ of _____ for the local charities and serve food for a _____ in my _____ once a _____. It is _____ to _____ how many _____ cannot afford to _____. Unfortunately, the number of _____ _____ has _____ because of the coronavirus pandemic.

16. Faulty translation: correct the mistakes in the translation of paragraph 4 below (9 mistakes)

Unfortunately, I have been teaching Spanish for free to refugees for three years and I think that this experience is very sad. There are people from every part of Spain, and it is very exciting for me because I teach a lot about the culture and the customs of my countries of origin. This goes to show that when one takes, one always receives nothing in exchange.

17. Translate into English

a. Una asociación benéfica

b. Tener la oportunidad

c. Los productos de primera necesidad

d. Una experiencia muy enriquecedora

e. Tener éxito en la vida

f. Siempre recibes algo a cambio

g. A causa de

h. Estoy de guardia

i. El número ha aumentado

TEXT 2 – Lola (20 años, Jerez)

(1) Hago trabajo voluntario en mi barrio todos los domingos y me encanta porque me siento útil y me permite conocer a gente *[to meet people]*. A mi parecer, es necesario luchar contra la pobreza, así que para ayudar, sirvo comida en un comedor social una vez a la semana. Es una locura ver el número de personas que hoy en día no tienen los medios *[don't have the means]* para comprar comida.

(2) Creo que es nuestra responsabilidad no olvidarnos de aquellos que tienen necesidades y por eso me gusta ofrecer mi tiempo para ayudar a los demás. A veces también hago donaciones de dinero a diversas organizaciones benéficas, porque desafortunadamente solo el tiempo no es suficiente y hace falta también medios financieros para alimentar y acomodar a los sin techo.

(3) Además, desde hace cuatro años soy voluntario en una asociación benéfica para ayudar a los sin techo. En primer lugar, ayudamos a las personas a encontrar alojamiento temporal en la ciudad, y luego les ayudamos a encontrar trabajo. El objetivo de esta asociación es reintegrar a las personas en la sociedad y ofrecerles ayuda a la hora de solicitar trabajos.

(4) Tengo que decir que la asociación tiene mucho éxito y dos de cada tres personas encuentran su camino a la independencia económica gracias a nuestra ayuda. En el futuro, me gustaría ofrecer mi apoyo a las personas mayores, porque pienso que es uno de los sectores de la sociedad más vulnerables de nuestros días y tenemos la tendencia a descuidarlos.

18. Complete the following sentences from the paragraphs 1, 2 and 3 then translate them into English

a. Hago trabajo _____ (1)

b. Me _____ conocer a gente (1)

c. _____ contra la pobreza (1)

d. Sirvo comida en un _____ social (1)

e. No olvidarnos de aquellos que tienen _____ (2)

f. Hago _____ de dinero (2)

g. Para _____ y acomodar a los sin techo (2)

h. Encontrar alojamiento _____ en la ciudad (3)

i. Reintegrar a las personas en la _____ (3)

19. Complete the sentences below based on paragraphs 2 and 3

a. It is our responsibility not to _____

b. I like to offer _____

c. Sometimes, I also make _____

d. We need the financial means to feed and _____ homeless people

e. Thus, I have also _____ for the last four years

f. Firstly, we help_____, and then _____

g. The association's goal is to reintegrate these people back into society and _____

20. Complete the translation of paragraph 4

I have to _____ that the association has a lot of success and _____ out of _____ people find their _____ to economic _____ thanks to our _____. In the _____, I would like to _____ my support to _____ people, because I think that it is one of the most _____ categories of our population _____ and we tend to neglect _____.

21. Find in the text the Spanish equivalent for the following

e.g. *To meet*: **C**onocer

a. *To feed:* A

b. *Volunteer:* V

c. *Means:* M

d. *Path:* C

e. *To help:* A

f. *Necessary:* N

g. *To find:* E

h. *Donations:* D

i. *Accommodation:* A

j. *Roof:* T

k. *To apply for a job:* S

22. Complete the text with the options provided

Hago trabajo voluntario en mi _____ todos los domingos y me encanta porque me siento _____ y me permite _____ a gente. A mi parecer, es necesario luchar contra la _____, así que para ayudar, sirvo comida en un comedor _____ una vez a la semana. Es una locura ver el _____ de personas que hoy en día no tienen los _____ para comprar comida. Creo que es nuestra responsabilidad no _____ de aquellos que tienen _____ y por eso me gusta ofrecer mi tiempo para ayudar a los demás. A veces también hago donaciones de dinero a diversas organizaciones _____, porque desafortunadamente solo el tiempo no es _____ y hace falta también medios financieros para alimentar y _____ a los sin techo.

medios	útil	suficiente	social	benéficas	conocer
pobreza	acomodar	olvidarnos	necesidades	barrio	número

23. Tiled translation: translate the text below using the chunks of language provided in the table

I believe that it is essential to fight against poverty and social inequalities in general. We must support the people in need. Therefore, I do a lot of charity work. At least three times a week. Once a week, on Mondays, I serve food in a soup kitchen. On Wednesdays, I do homework help in a neighbouring school. On Fridays, I help the homeless. I have been a volunteer in a charity for homeless people for three years. I like this a lot because I feel useful. In the future, I would like to provide assistance to disabled children and the elderly.

comedor social.	las desigualdades	y ancianos.	He sido voluntario en una	personas que lo	Los viernes ayudo a
hago mucho	siento útil.	Esto me gusta mucho	organización	sociales en general.	Los miércoles
En el futuro,	Una vez a la	necesitan.	me gustaría	Al menos tres veces	escuela del barrio.
benéfica para personas	luchar contra	trabajo de caridad.	Creo que es fundamental	a niños discapacitados	sirvo comidas en un
a la semana.	deberes en una	Debemos apoyar a las	ayudo con los	semana, los lunes,	sin hogar durante
Por lo tanto,	tres años.	ofrecer asistencia	los sin techo.	porque me	la pobreza y

24. Translate into Spanish

a. I help the homeless

b. In my neighbourhood

c. To fight against

d. It is necessary

e. Money donations

f. To reduce poverty

g. To lower unemployment

h. To support the elderly

i. To provide assistance

j. In my school

25. Split sentences

1	2	English translation
Es nuestra responsabilidad	sirvo comida a los sin techo	
Me gusta porque	contra las desigualdades	
Ayudo a los	muy enriquecedora	
Muchas personas no tienen	imprescindible reducir el paro	
Es importante luchar	de ropa en mi barrio	
En el futuro quiero apoyar	niños a hacer sus deberes	
Hago donaciones	me siento útil	
Es una experiencia	a los refugiados	
Creo que es	ayudar a los descapacitados	
Todos los martes	medios para comprar comida	

26. Guided English-to-Spanish translation (try to do as much of it as possible from memory)

a. *People in need*   L__ g_____ n_____

b. *For three years*   D_____ t_____ a_____

c. *I volunteer*   H_____ u_ v_____

d. *In the future*   E_ e_ f_____

e. *I like that a lot*   M_ g_____ m_____

f. *In order to help*   P____ a_____

g. *I would like to help the poor*

M_ g_____ a_____ a l__ p_____

h. *For refugees*   Para l___ r_____

i. *In a charity*   E_ u__ asoc_____ ben_____

j. *I serve food*   S_____ c_____

k. *The most destitute*   L__ m__ n_____

l. *We must help*   D_____ a_____

m. *To fight against*   L_____ c_____

n. *I make money donations*

H_____ d_____ d_ d_____

27. Translate into Spanish

a. I help in a charity in my town each week

b. I do volunteer work in my neighbourhood every Sunday

c. I feel useful when I help others, which is important for me

d. I believe it's essential to fight poverty

e. We must help the most destitute

f. I help the homeless to find accommodation

g. To help, I make money donations and I serve food in a soup kitchen every weekend

h. In the future, I would like to provide assistance to the elderly

28. Write a 120 words composition including the following points

- Talk about what volunteer work you do in your town, neighbourhood or school
- Say how you feel about this work and why
- Say why it's important to help others
- Mention what you would like to do in the future to help

Key questions

¿Eres voluntario/a para una organización benéfica? En caso afirmativo, ¿desde cuándo?	*Are you a volunteer for a charity? If yes, since how long?*
¿Qué haces para ayudar a los demás?	*What do you do to help others?*
¿Qué opinas de hacer trabajo voluntario?	*What do you think about volunteering?*
¿Por qué es importante ayudar a las personas necesitadas?	*Why is it important to help people in need?*
¿Cómo ayudas a las personas desfavorecidas de tu ciudad?	*How do you help the underprivileged in your town?*
En el futuro, ¿qué tipo de voluntariado te gustaría hacer? ¿Por qué?	*In the future, what type of volunteering would you like to do? Why?*

Unit 7. Charity and voluntary work (future tense)

La semana que viene *Next week*	**está en mis planes** *I am planning to*	**ayudar en una organización benéfica** *help in a charity*	**en mi barrio** *in my neighbourhood*
El próximo verano *Next summer*	**me gustaría** *I would like to*	**ayudar en una ONG** *help in an NGO*	**en mi calle** *in my street*
Las próximas vacaciones *Next holidays*	**tengo la intención de** *I intend to*	**hacer trabajo voluntario** *do volunteer work*	**en mi pueblo** *in my village*

Me hace ilusión *I'm looking forward to it*	**porque tendré la oportunidad de** *because I will have the chance to*	**ayudar a los demás** *help others*
Creo que me gustará *I think I will like it*		**sentirme útil** *feel useful*
		ser generoso/a *be generous*

Será *It will be*	**una buena oportunidad para** *a good opportunity to*	**combatir** *fight*	**el hambre** *starvation*
		reducir *lower*	**el paro** *unemployment*
	muy alentador *very uplifting*	**luchar contra** *fight against*	**la pobreza** *poverty*
			las desigualdades *inequalities*

Lo que más me interesa es *What I am most interested in is*	**apoyar a** *to support*	**los pobres** *poor people*
	ayudar a *to help*	**los más desfavorecidos** *the most destitute*
	echar una mano a *to lend a hand to*	**los sin techo** *the homeless*

Es nuestro deber *It is our duty*	**no ignorar** *to not ignore*	**a las personas más necesitadas** *people in need*
Es nuestra responsabilidad *It is our responsibility*	**no olvidar** *to not forget*	**a los desfavorecidos** *the underprivileged*

En el futuro *In future*	**haré donaciones de dinero** *I will make money donations*	**a las organizaciones benéficas locales** *to local charities*
	serviré comida *I will serve food*	**en un comedor social** *in a soup kitchen*

Además, *Furthermore,*	**daré clases gratuitas de inglés** *I will give free English lessons*	**para los indigentes** *for the destitute*
Asimismo, *Additionally,*	**haré trabajo voluntario en una asociación** *I will volunteer in an association*	**para refugiados** *for refugees*

Si tuviera más tiempo, *If I had had more time,*	**me gustaría ayudar a** *I would like to help*	**los niños discapacitados** *disabled childen*
Si pudiera, *If I could,*	**también apoyaría a** *I would also support*	**las personas mayores** *the elderly*

1. Match

La semana que viene	I will feel useful
El paro	It will be an opportunity
En un comedor social	I would like
Los niños discapacitados	Unemployment
Haré trabajo voluntario	Money donations
Ayudaré en una ONG	Next week
Será una oportunidad	In a soup kitchen
Me sentiré útil	Disabled children
Las donaciones de dinero	I will volunteer
Me gustaría	I will help in an NGO

2. Complete the words then translate them into English

a. Desigu_ _ _ _ _ _ _

b. Alen_ _ _ _ _

c. Serv_ _

d. En mi pu_ _ _ _

e. Tengo la int_ _ _ _ _ _

f. Daré clases grat_ _ _ _ _

g. Asociación para los indi_ _ _ _ _ _

h. Oportunidad para com_ _ _ _ _

i. Las próximas vac_ _ _ _ _ _ _

j. Es nuestro de_ _ _

3. Phrase puzzle

a. comida Serviré   *I will serve food*

b. de Daré inglés clases   *I will teach English*

c. verano próximo El   *Next summer*

d. personas Las necesitadas más   *People in need*

e. tuviera Si tiempo más   *If I had more time*

f. benéfica Una asociación *A charity*

g. Los techo sin   *Homeless people*

h. me Creo gustará que   *I think I will like it*

i. intención la Tengo de   *I intend to*

j. el haré futuro En   *In future I will do*

4. Complete with the missing words

a. En mi _____   *In my neighbourhood*

b. _____ una mano a   *To lend a hand to*

c. Es nuestro deber no _____   *It is our duty to not ignore*

d. _____ comida   *I will serve food*

e. Los _____   *The underprivileged*

f. Me _____ ilusión   *I'm looking forward to*

g. ____ una oportunidad para *It will be an opportunity to*

h. Si _____ más tiempo   *If I had more time*

i. Me _____ ayudar   *I would like to help*

j. _____ la pobreza   *To fight poverty*

5. Complete the text below with the options provided in the table

El próximo verano _____ en mis planes hacer _____ voluntario en ___ barrio. _____ clases de _____ gratuitas a los niños _____. También __ gustaría _____ a los mayores. Si _____ más tiempo _____ comida a los_____, pero de momento haré _____ de dinero a un comedor social.

donaciones	trabajo	mi	refugiados
me	tuviera	está	inglés
daré	apoyar	desfavorecidos	serviría

Conversación entre amigos (1) (Part 1)

Lola: ¿Está en tus planes hacer un voluntariado en alguna asociación benéfica?

Mateo: Sí, daré clases gratuitas de español a refugiados este verano. Hay una organización benéfica en mi barrio.

Lola: ¿Crees que te gustará?

Mateo: Sí, estoy seguro de que será una experiencia muy enriquecedora *[rewarding]*. Habrá personas de todo el mundo y seguramente será muy interesante para mí. Me hace ilusión porque aprenderé mucho de su cultura y las costumbres de sus países de origen.

Lola: ¿Te gustaría hacer algo más?

Mateo: Sí, la semana que viene ayudaré un poco con los deberes de los estudiantes de mi antigua universidad. Me gusta mucho porque me siento útil y gracias a esas clases conoceré más gente joven y simpática.

6. Find the Spanish for the following words or expressions

a. To volunteer in a

b. To refugees this summer

c. I will learn a lot

d. Very rewarding

e. I'm looking forward to

f. Customs from their countries

g. People from all over the world

h. Would you like…?

i. Next week

j. My old university

k. Young people

l. Nice

m. Anything else

7. Answer in English

a. When will Mateo be teaching Spanish and to whom?

b. How does he think he will find this experience?

c. Where will his students be from?

d. What will he learn himself?

e. What will he do next week?

f. Where will that happen?

g. How does he feel about this experience?

h. Who will he meet?

8. Tangled translation: into Spanish

a. Daré clases *free* a los *refugees* este *summer*

b. *A* asociación *charity* en mi *neighbourhood*

c. Aprenderé *a lot* de su *culture* y las *customs*

d. De sus *countries* de *origin*

e. ¿Te gustaría *do anything* más?

f. Los *students* de mi *old* universidad

g. Será una *experience* muy *rewarding*

h. *Thanks* a esas clases *I will meet* a más *people*

9. Faulty translation: spot the errors in the English translations below and correct

a. La semana que viene haré una donación de dinero a un comedor social en mi ciudad
Last week, I will make a clothes donation to a charity in my town

b. En el futuro me gustaría ayudar a las personas mayores desfavorecidas
In the future I will help disabled elderly people

c. Creo que es nuestro deber no olvidar a los sin techo y ayudarles a encontrar hogar
I believe that it is their responsibility to forget the homeless people and help them to find food

Conversación entre amigos (1) (Part 2)

Lola: En tu opinión, ¿por qué es importante ayudar a las personas necesitadas?

Mateo: Siempre he pensado que es muy importante luchar contra las desigualdades y que todos deberían *[should]* tener la oportunidad de vivir, comer y estudiar decentemente. Por eso me gustaría involucrarme *[get involved]*. Pero a veces el tiempo no es suficiente. Por eso, mañana donaré dinero a un comedor social en mi ciudad y por la noche, ayudaré a servir comida ahí.

Lola: ¿Cómo crees que será esta experiencia?

Mateo: Por una parte me hace ilusión ayudar a los desfavorecidos, pero por otra parte sé que será duro ver a tanta gente sin recursos para vivir de forma digna. Desafortunadamente, recientemente la cantidad de personas pobres ha aumentado debido a la pandemia de coronavirus.

11. Find the Spanish for the following expressions

a. I have always thought

b. I would like to get involved

c. I will donate money

d. I will help to serve food

e. On the one hand I'm looking forward to

f. So many people without means

g. The amount of poor people has increased

h. To live with dignity

13. Translate the following verbs into Spanish

a. They should

b. I would like

c. I will donate

d. I will help

e. It will be

f. Has increased

g. I'm looking forward to

h. I have thought

10. Answer in English

a. What does Mateo think everyone should have the opportunity to do decently? (3 details)

b. Apart from getting involved, what else will he do?

c. What will he do tomorrow evening?

d. How does he think he will find this experience?

e. Which factor has increased the number of poor people recently?

f. What is the phrase for "on the one hand" in Spanish?

12. Complete the translation from Mateo's second answer

On the one hand, I am _____ to help the _____, but on the other hand I _____ that it will be _____ to see so many people without the _____ to live with dignity. Unfortunately, the amount of _____ people has _____ increased due to the coronavirus _____.

14. Answer the following questions to the best of your ability using the Sentence Builder from this unit and the conversation above for support. Then practice with a partner.

a. ¿Te gustaría ofrecer tu tiempo como voluntario/a para una organización benéfica? Si es así, ¿cómo crees que sería?

b. Si tuvieras más tiempo, ¿a quién te gustaría ayudar primero? ¿Por qué?

c. ¿Crees que podrías ayudar a otros estudiantes en tu universidad? Si es así, ¿cómo?

d. ¿Crees que podrías aprender algo ayudando a los demás?

e. ¿Crees que es importante involucrarse de esta manera?

THE LANGUAGE GYM

Conversación entre amigos (2)

Jerónimo: Hola Clara, cuéntame ¿cómo te imaginas la experiencia de hacer un voluntariado?

Clara: Hola Jerónimo. Tendré mi primera oportunidad de hacer un voluntariado en las próximas vacaciones.

Jerónimo: ¿Y te hace ilusión?

Clara: ¡Sí! Tengo muchas ganas de empezar ya. Creo que esa experiencia me permitirá conocer a mucha gente de otros barrios de mi ciudad. Para ayudar, una vez a la semana serviré comida en un comedor social. Me imagino que veré a muchas personas que no pueden permitirse comprar comida.

Jerónimo: ¿Crees que es importante ayudar a los pobres?

Clara: Sí, por supuesto. Es nuestra responsabilidad no olvidar a las personas necesitadas. Me siento útil cuando puedo ayudar a los demás. El mes que viene donaré dinero a varias organizaciones benéficas. Desafortunadamente, el tiempo no es suficiente. Necesitamos organizarnos mejor para alimentar a aquellos que no tienen la suerte de tener medios para permitirse comer dignamente todos los días.

Jerónimo: Pues, buena suerte. Espero que te vaya bien.

15. Gapped translation

a. ¿Cómo te _____? *How do you imagine*

b. _____ un voluntariado *To volunteer*

c. Tengo muchas _____ *I can't wait*

d. Mi primera _____ *My first opportunity*

e. _____ comida *I will serve food*

f. _____ gente *A lot of people*

g. Me _____ que *I imagine that*

h. _____ a los demás *To help others*

i. Sí, por _____ *Yes, of course*

j. Organizaciones _____ *Charities*

k. El _____ … *Time…*

l. …no es _____ *…is not enough*

m. _____ *To organize ourselves*

n. _____ *To feed*

o. _____ comer todos los días
To allow oneself to eat every day

16. Answer in English

a. Where will Clara work as a volunteer next holiday?

b. What will she do?

c. How is she feeling about it? (2 details)

d. What does she think she will see?

e. What's the verb for "to forget" in Spanish?

f. How do we say "luck" in Spanish?

g. How would you say "good luck" to someone?

h. What's the verb for "to feed" in Spanish?

i. What does she think we could do better?

17. Turn the following verbs into the future tense, then translate into English

Present	Future tense	English
Hago		
Ayudo		
Veo		
Es		
Sirvo		
Tengo		
Doy		

18. Challenge: translate the following paragraph into English

Estoy seguro de que la organización benéfica en mi barrio tendrá mucho éxito y, por lo menos, dos de cada tres personas lograrán la independencia financiera gracias a nuestra ayuda. Si tuviera más tiempo, también me gustaría apoyar a las personas mayores, porque pienso que son uno de las grupos más vulnerables de nuestra sociedad y, desafortunadamente, tendemos a olvidarnos de ellos.

Key questions

¿Está en tus planes hacer trabajo voluntario para una organización benéfica? Si es así, ¿cómo crees que será?	*Are you planning to volunteer for a charity? If yes, how do you think it will be?*
¿Qué podrás hacer para ayudar a los demás en el futuro?	*What could you do to help others next week?*
¿Qué te parece la idea de hacer trabajo voluntario?	*What did you think about the idea of volunteer work?*
¿Cómo puedes ayudar a las personas desfavorecidas de tu barrio?	*How can you help the underprivileged in your neighbourhood?*
Si tuvieras más tiempo, ¿a quién te gustaría ayudar primero? ¿Por qué?	*If you had more time, who would you like to help first? Why?*

Unit 8. Homelessness (present tense)

Los indigentes *The destitute* / Los sin techo *The homeless*	son personas	pobres/vulnerables	que suelen vivir	en la calle / en albergues

En invierno *In winter*		pueden dormir en *they can sleep in*	centros de acogida *homeless shelters*
Durante los meses *During the ... months*	**más duros** *harshest* / **más fríos** *coldest*	**pueden encontrar refugio en** *they can find refuge in* / **tienen acceso a** *they have access to*	**albergues** *refuges*

Para alimentarse *To feed themselves* / Para salir adelante *To cope* / Para sobrevivir *To survive*	a veces / en ocasiones	necesitan *they need to* / se ven obligados a *they are forced to* / tienen que *they must*	buscar en los contenedores *to rummage through the bins* / buscarse la vida *to manage by themselves* / pedir limosna *to beg* / robar *steal*

En algunos casos *In some cases* / En el peor de los casos *In the worst of cases*	duermen *they sleep* / se refugian *they take shelter*	en los cajeros automáticos *in the ATMs* / en las estaciones de tren *in train stations* / en la calle *on the street*

La exclusión *Exclusion* / La pobreza *Poverty* / La soledad *Lonelines* / La falta de higiene *The lack of hygiene* / Vivir en la calle *Living on the street*	puede causar problemas *can cause problems* / puede llevar a conflictos *can lead to issues*	de abuso de alcohol *of alcohol abuse* / de adicción a *of addiction to* / de alcoholismo *of alcoholism* / de salud (mental) *of (mental) health* / sociales *social (issues/problems etc)*

Los sin techo *The homeless* / Los que viven en la calle *Those living on the street*	se exponen al riesgo de *are exposed to the risk of* / son a menudo víctimas *are often victims*	de humillaciones verbales *of verbal humiliation* / de violencia física *of physical violence*

Es nuestro deber *It is our duty* / Es nuestra responsabilidad *It is our responsibility*	ayudarles a *to help them (to)* / echarles una mano para *to give them a helping hand (to)*	encontrar un hogar *to find a home* / independizarse *become independent* / reinsertarse en la sociedad *to reintegrate into society*

*Author's note An 'indigente' is someone who would typically be found on the street, perhaps sleeping rough, and sometimes begging for money. A 'sin techo' is a homeless person, but there is no implication that they are necessarily begging for money, they have just lost their home. The word 'indigente' does not carry a positive/negative connotation in Spanish, unlike the English 'tramp'/'beggar', which are slightly loaded terms.

1. Match

Abuso de alcohol	Our duty
Centros de acogida	In order to cope
En la calle	Alcohol abuse
Durante los meses	To beg
Echar una mano	Homeless shelters
Salud	Poor people
Alimentarse	They live
Para salir adelante	On the street
Pedir limosna	Health
Gente pobre	During the months
Los sin techo	They sleep
Nuestro deber	To give a hand
Duermen	To feed themselves
Viven	The homeless

2. Choose the correct option

a. Los **sin /con** techo — *The homeless*

b. En **primavera/invierno** — *In winter*

c. **Viven/duermen** — *They live*

d. **Echar/Ayudar** una mano — *To give a hand*

e. En **la calle/el cajero** — *On the street*

f. Es nuestro **deber/poder** — *It is our duty*

g. Los **centros de acogida/salud** *Homeless shelters*

h. La falta de **pobreza/higiene** *The lack of hygiene*

i. **Buscar/ir** en los contenedores
To rummage through bins

j. Se **encuentran/exponen** al riesgo
Theu are exposed to the risk

k. Los meses más **duros/fríos**
The harshest months

3. Phrase puzzle

a. veces La de mayoría las — *Most of the time*

b. sin Los techo — *The homeless*

c. La higiene de falta — *The lack of hygiene*

d. de Los centros acogida — *Homeless shelters*

e. En tren pasillos los de estación la de — *In the corridors of a train station*

f. en Fuera la calle — *Outside on the street*

g. sociedad en Reinsertarse la — *To reintegrate into society*

h. Los alcohol abuso problemas de de — *Problems of alcohol abuse*

i. Pueden en refugio encontrar — *They can find refuge in*

4. Gapped Words

a. L_s p_br_s — *The poor*

b. _bl_g_d_ — *Forced*

c. _lb_rg__ — *Shelter*

d. _nv__rn_ — *Winter*

e. R__sg_ — *Risk*

f. D_b_r — *Duty*

g. Co_t_n_do_es — *Bins*

h. S_l_d_d — *Loneliness*

i. S_br_v_v_r — *To survive*

5. Gapped translation

a. Durante los meses fríos — *During the _____ months*

b. Vivir en las calles — *_____ on the street*

c. El riesgo de humillaciones verbales — *The risk of verbal _____*

d. En ocasiones se ven obligados — *Sometimes they are _____*

e. Puede llevar a conflictos — *It can _____ to issues*

f. Necesitan pedir limosna — *They need to _____*

g. Víctima de la violencia física — *Victim of _____ violence*

6. Break the flow (phrases)

a. Puedenencontrarrefugioenalbergues

b. Echarlesunamanoparaencontrarcasa

c. Duermenenloscajeros

d. Buscarenloscontenedores

e. Seexponenalriesgo

f. Reinsertarseenlasociedad

g. Problemasdesaludmental

7. Complete with the options provided

a. Los indigentes son personas _____ que suelen vivir en la calle

b. En invierno tienen acceso a los centros de _____

c. Para _____ a veces buscan comida en los contenedores

d. La exclusión puede _____ problemas de salud mental

e. A veces los ___ techo duermen en las estaciones de tren

f. La pobreza puede llevar a problemas de _____

g. Para salir _____ se ven obligados a _____ la vida

h. La gente pobre se _____ al riesgo de violencia física y humillaciones _____

sobrevivir	buscarse	adicción	acogida	sin
expone	vulnerables	verbales	adelante	causar

8. Missing letter challenge

a. En inv_erno

b. Alberg_e

c. Humi_lación verbal

d. La exclusi_n

e. Indepen_izarse

f. Encontrar refu_io en

g. Pedir li_osna

h. La falta de h_giene

i. D_ermen

j. _enerar conflictos

k. Los c_jeros

9. Spot the missing words: there are two missing in each sentence

a. Durante meses más duros pueden dormir los centros de acogida

b. Para salir adelante, a veces, se obligados a pedir limosna o incluso, en el de los casos, a robar comida

c. Es nuestra responsabilidad echarles una para reinsertarse la sociedad y encontrar un hogar

d. La soledad la exclusión pueden llevar a problemas salud mental

e. Los indigentes personas pobres y vulnerables suelen dormir en la calle

f. Los techo son a menudo víctimas violencia física y de humillaciones verbales

g. En invierno los más pobres duermen en calle, las estaciones tren o incluso en los cajeros

10. Translate into English

a. La mayoría de las veces

b. Los sin techo

c. La falta de higiene

d. Los centros de acogida

e. Encontrar un hogar

f. Independizarse

g. Nuestro deber

h. Los problemas de abuso de alcohol

i. Personas vulnerables

j. Encontrar refugio

k. Viven

l. Durante los meses más fríos

m. Conflictos sociales

n. Buscarse la vida

o. La exclusión

p. Para sobrevivir

q. Tienen acceso a

r. Se exponen al riesgo de

s. La pobreza y la soledad

t. Echarles una mano

11. Gapped translation

a. __ sin techo son gente _____   *The homeless are poor people*

b. _____ son muy vulnerables   *They are also very vulnerable*

c. __ invierno pueden dormir en los centros de_____   *In winter they can sleep in homeless shelters*

d. Sin embargo, a _____ duermen en la _____   *However, they often sleep on the street*

e. A _____ duermen en las _____ de tren   *Sometimes, they sleep in the train stations*

f. Para _____ se ___ obligados a pedir limosna   *To survive they are forced to beg*

g. Vivir __ la calle _____ llevar a conflictos sociales   *Living on the street can lead to social issues*

h. _____ veces, para salir _____, tienen que buscar en los _____
Many times, to cope, they must rummage through bins

12. Sentence puzzle

a. Los humillaciones sin se exponen al riesgo verbales techo de
The homeless are exposed to the risk of verbal humiliation

b. menudo La violencia pobre gente víctima a es de física
The poor people are often victims of physical violence

c. Para buscar contenedores se ven sobrevivir obligados a en los
To survive, they are forced to rummage through bins

d. peor Tienen en que pedir casos robar limosna o incluso, el de los,
They have to beg or even, in the worst of cases, steal

e. Es decente echarles una mano para encontrar un necesario hogar
It is necessary to give them a hand to find decent accommodation

f. buscarse Tienen vida que la
They have to manage by themselves

g. Muy fríos incluso a menudo calle duermen en la, en los meses más
Very often, they sleep on the street, even during the coldest months

13. Tangled translation: into Spanish

a. La *lack of* higiene *can* causar los problemas de *health*

b. *To* alimentarse se ven *forced* a buscar en la *bins*

c. Es *our* responsabilidad echarles una *hand* para independizarse

d. Durante los *months* más *cold* a menudo *they sleep* en las estaciones de tren y a veces *ATMs*

e. Los sin *roof* son gente *poor* y vulnerable

f. *The* exclusión puede *cause* conflictos sociales y *lead* a adicciones

g. Los *destitute* son a menudo víctimas de *humiliations* verbales

h. Debemos *help them* a *find* un *home* decente

14. Translate into Spanish

a. The homeless

b. Alcohol abuse

c. Poverty

d. The lack of hygiene

e. To give a helping hand

f. Outside on the street

g. They need

h. They are forced to

i. To rummage through bins

TEXT 1 – David (22 años, Pontevedra)

(1) Los sin techo son, por definición, gente sin hogar. A menudo, por falta de dinero, duermen en la calle, debajo de un puente o en los pasillos de una estación. Para salir adelante, tienen que pedir limosna o buscar en los contenedores para encontrar algo de comer o para vestirse [to dress].

(2) Para sobrevivir, se ven obligados a buscarse la vida solos y vivir el día a día, a menudo buscando cualquier oportunidad. En invierno, durante los meses más duros, por lo general tienen acceso a centros de acogida que les ayudan a encontrar alojamiento durante la temporada de frío.

(3) Desafortunadamente, la exclusión puede causar problemas de alcoholismo, que igualmente, pueden llevar a problemas graves de salud. El aislamiento y la falta de domicilio fijo puede causar problemas de sociabilidad, entre los que se encuentran el rechazo de toda ayuda exterior y no querer mezclarse con otras personas.

(4) La generación actual de pobres se expone al riesgo de humillaciones verbales de manera cotidiana y también a menudo son víctimas de la violencia física. Los gobiernos de los países del mundo entero deberían hacer más para ayudarlos y es nuestro deber colectivo echarles una mano para que encuentren un hogar decente y puedan reinsertarse en la sociedad.

15. Find the Spanish equivalent in paragraphs 1 and 2

a. Homeless people

b. Lack of money

c. They sleep

d. Under a bridge

e. To beg

f. Rummage through bins

g. In order to find

h. They are forced to

i. To manage by themselves

j. Homeless shelters

16. Complete the translation of paragraph 3

_____, exclusion can _____ problems of alcoholism, which equally, can _____ to serious _____ problems. The isolation and the lack of _____ address can also _____ troubles of sociability which include _____ all external _____ and not _____ to mix with other _____.

17. Place a tick next to the words below which are contained in paragraph 4, and cross the ones which aren't

a. new	e. world	i. rich
b. to give	f. society	j. daily
c. cause	g. often	k. outside
d. but	h. loneliness	l. try

18. Complete the sentence below based on the text

a. By definition, the homeless are _____

b. Due to lack of money, they _____

c. To cope, they must _____

d. Social centres help them _____

e. The isolation can cause _____

f. Some of them refuse _____

g. They are exposed to the risk of _____ on a daily basis

19. Find the Spanish in paragraph 4

a. The current generation:

b. Is exposed to the risk:

c. Daily (3 words):

d. Are victims of physical violence:

e. Our collective duty:

f. To give them a hand:

g. To find a decent home:

h. To reintegrate themselves into society:

TEXT 2 – Raúl (23 años, Burgos)

(1) Una persona sin hogar es alguien, que no tiene casa ni lugar para vivir, y por tanto, es una persona que vive en la calle y que duerme donde puede. Algunos lugares comunes donde duermen los sin techo (cuando no pueden acceder a centros de acogida) son cajeros automáticos, las estaciones de trenes o debajo de puentes, por ejemplo.

(2) Varios términos se utilizan en el lenguaje cotidiano para hablar de estas personas en los márgenes de la sociedad. Algunos nombres, como "vagabundo" o incluso "mendigo" pueden ser peyorativos. Para sobrevivir, estas personas vulnerables deben buscarse la vida y vivir al día.

(3) La precariedad y la insalubridad (suciedad) pueden llevar a problemas de salud y, lamentablemente, cada invierno, muchas personas sin hogar mueren de frío en las calles. Estas personas también son muy a menudo víctimas de humillaciones verbales y, a veces, incluso de violencia física.

(4) A pesar de los esfuerzos de muchas organizaciones benéficas, así como de muchos individuos, algunos ciudadanos aún se quedan atrás y deben superar obstáculos diarios para lograr cubrir necesidades básicas. Los sin techo no tienen acceso a una vivienda, alimentación, un sistema de salud digno, educación y, mucho menos, trabajo.

(5) Es un hecho triste, pero es la dura realidad de nuestra sociedad moderna y es nuestra responsabilidad colectiva echarles una mano para reinsertarse en la sociedad.

20. Find the Spanish equivalent in paragraphs 1 & 2

a. A homeless person

b. A person who lives on the street

c. He/She sleeps where he/she can

d. When they can't access homeless shelters

e. ATMs

f. Daily language

g. They can be pejorative (rude/disrespectful)

h. Some names

i. Like "vagabond" or even "tramp"

j. To survive

k. These vulnerable people

l. Manage by themselves

m. To live from day to day

21. Answer the questions below about paragraph 3, 4 and 5

a. What causes health problems?

b. What happens every winter?

c. What also happens, very often to the homeless?

d. Who is making an effort to help the homeless?

e. What basic necessities are listed in paragraph 4?

f. What is our collective responsibility?

22. Correct the following phrases which have been copied wrongly from the text

a. Una person sin hogar es algun que no tiene casa

b. Dormen en las estaciones trénes

c. Estos personas vulnerables deben buscar la vida

d. Cada inverno, muchas persona sin hogar muere de frío

e. Les sin techó no tener acceso a vivienda

f. Es un hecha triste, pero está la dura realidad

23. Translate into English the following words/phrases from paragraph 5

a. Un hecho triste

b. La dura realidad

c. Nuestra sociedad moderna

d. Nuestra responsabilidad colectiva

e. Echarles una mano

f. Para reinsertarse

g. A la sociedad

24. Complete with the options provided

Los sin techo son, por definición, gente sin_____. A menudo, por falta de dinero, _____ en la calle, debajo de un puente o en los pasillos de una estación. Para salir _____, tienen que pedir limosna o buscar en los _____ para encontrar algo de comer o para _____.

Para _____, están obligados a buscarse la _____ solos y vivir el día a día, a menudo _____ cualquier _____. En invierno, durante los meses más duros, por lo general tienen acceso a _____ de urgencia o centros de acogida que les ayudan a encontrar _____ para la temporada de _____.

duermen	alojamiento	sobrevivir	buscando	frío	adelante
vida	vestirse	contenedores	oportunidad	hogar	refugios

25. Tiled translation: translate the text below using the chunks of language provided in the table

Homeless people are very poor and vulnerable people who live in terrible conditions.

They tend to sleep on the street, under a bridge or in the corridors of a train station.

They have lost everything and lack the means to feed or dress themselves. They are forced to manage by themselves and to live from day to day.

In order to survive, they sometimes rummage through bins and beg and, in the worst case scenario, steal. The lack of hygiene can lead to serious diseases and the loneliness can cause mental health issues, addictions and alcoholism.

During winter, many of them die sleeping outside in the cold.

son personas muy	salud mental,	Se ven obligados a	adicciones y
solos y vivir	en la calle,	sin hogar	de una estación de tren.
y la soledad	por el frío.	alcoholismo.	invierno, muchos de
alimentarse	contenedores, piden limosna y,	viven en	higiene puede
a veces buscan en los	los pasillos	durmiendo al aire libre	puente o en
pobres y vulnerables que	buscarse la vida	puede causar	Para sobrevivir,
condiciones terribles.	Durante el	enfermedades graves	llevar a
Suelen dormir	La falta de	Lo han perdido	Las personas
problemas de	ni vestirse.	en el peor de los casos, roban.	los medios para
todo y no tienen	ellos mueren	debajo de un	el día al día.

26. Split phrases form logical sentences joining bits from each column

Los sin techo son	que pedir limosna o incluso, en el peor de los casos, robar
Muy a menudo, durante el	dormir en los centros de acogida
Para salir adelante tienen	de alcoholismo y adicciones
Es nuestra responsabilidad echarles	son a menudo víctimas de abusos verbales
Durante los meses más fríos pueden	obligados a buscar comida en los contenedores
La falta de higiene puede	invierno, duermen en las estaciones de tren
Vivir en la calle puede llevar a problemas	causar problemas de salud
Desafortunadamente, la gente pobre	personas pobres y vulnerables
Para alimentarse se ven	una mano para reinsertarse en la sociedad

27. Complete with the missing verb

a. Es nuestro deber ayudarles a e_ _ _ _ _ _ _ _ un hogar decente

b. Para s_ _ _ _ _ _ _ _ _, en ocasiones, tienen que buscarse la vida

c. En invierno los indigentes p_ _ _ _ _ encontrar refugio en los albergues

d. La exclusión puede c_ _ _ _ _ problemas de salud mental

e. Los que viven en la calle se e_ _ _ _ _ _ al riesgo de violencia física

f. La mayoría de las veces d_ _ _ _ _ _ en la calle o incluso en los cajeros

g. Los sin techo son personas vulnerables que s_ _ _ _ _ vivir en la calle

28. Translate into Spanish

a. *In the winter*   E_ i_____

b. *The homeless*   L___ s_ t_____

c. *Social centres*   L_ c_____ s_____

d. *Poor people*   L_ g_____ p_____

e. *A homeless shelter*   U_ c_____ d_ a_____

f. *To rummage through bins*   B_____ e_ l_ c_____

g. *On the street*   E_ l_ c_____

h. *Most of the time*   L_ m_____ d_ t_____

i. *Poverty*   L_ p_____

j. *The lack of hygiene*   L_ f_____ d_ h_____

k. *In train station*   E_ l_ e_____ d_ t____

l. *To manage by themselves*   B_____ l_ v_____

m. *Health problems*   L_ p_____ d_ s_____

29. Complete with a suitable word

a. Los sin _____

b. La _____ pobre

c. Durante los _____ más fríos

d. Los problemas de salud _____

e. La _____ de higiene

f. _____ una mano

g. _____ en la sociedad

h. Se exponen a _____

i. Para salir _____

j. Se _____ obligados

k. Pueden _____ refugio

l. Buscarse la _____

m. Tienen que encontrar un _____ decente

30. Tangled translation: into Spanish

a. Los *without* techo son gente *poor* y vulnerable

b. En *winter* tienen *access* a los *centres* de acogida

c. *Often* duermen *in* las estaciones de *train*

d. Durante los *months* más duros a veces mueren de *cold*

e. Para *survive* tienen que *rummage* en los *bins*

f. La *lack* de higiene puede *lead* a problemas de *health*

g. En el *worst* de los *cases,* se ven *forced* a *steal*

h. Los sin *roof* son *often* víctimas de violencia *physical*

31. Add in the missing words

a. ____ menudo

b. Tienen acceso _

c. Los problemas __ salud

d. __ exponen al riesgo de

e. ____ alimentarse

f. Los ___ techo

g. El abuso __ alcohol

h. Reinsertarse __ la sociedad

32. Translate into Spanish

a. In winter, some homeless people have access to social centres, others die of cold on the street.

b. In order to cope, they often need to beg or, in the worst of cases, steal.

c. They often sleep on the street, under a bridge or in train stations.

d. Exclusion and loneliness can cause mental health issues.

e. They are sometimes the victims of physical violence and verbal humiliation.

f. It is our collective duty to help them to find a decent accommodation.

g. They are vulnerable and poor people who have lost everything.

h. Once a week, I work for a charity. I serve food for the homeless in a soup kitchen in my town.

33. Translate the following paragraphs into Spanish

The homeless are vulnerable people. They are poor and live on the street in very difficult conditions. To survive, they have to rummage through bins, beg and sometimes, in the worst of cases, steal.

During the cold season, generally, they can sleep in emergency shelters, but some of them sleep on a bench in a park or in the corridors of a train station.

The lack of hygiene can lead to health issues, and loneliness can cause problems like alcoholism or other addictions.

Some of them have lost everything overnight *[de la noche a la mañana].* Outside, they are exposed to the risks of physical violence and verbal humiliation.

It is important to help them to reintegrate into society and to give them a helping hand to find decent accommodation.

34. Write 140 words including the following points

The living conditions of homeless people in your town

What they have to do in order to survive

The types of issues that their lifestyle generates

The difficulties they have to face on a daily basis

What you do to help

THE LANGUAGE GYM

Key questions

¿Cómo viven generalmente las personas sin hogar?	*How do homeless people generally live?*
¿Dónde duermen los sin techo?	*Where do the homeless sleep?*
¿Cómo sobreviven las personas sin hogar en las calles?	*How do the homeless survive on the street?*
¿Cómo podemos ayudar a las personas sin hogar?	*How can we help the homeless?*
¿A qué tipo de riesgos están expuestas las personas sin hogar?	*At what type of risks are the homeless exposed to?*
¿Cómo te quedas sin hogar?	*How does one become homeless?*
¿Cuáles son los problemas comunes relacionados con la vida sin hogar?	*What are the common problems linked to the homeless life?*

Unit 8. Homelessness (imperfect)

Cuando era más joven *When I was younger*	Cuando era pequeño *When I was growing up*

Recuerdo que había *I remember that there were*	algunos *some* más *more* menos *less*	indigentes *destitute (people)* sin techo *homeless (people)*	en el centro *in the city centre* en mi ciudad *in my city*

En invierno *In winter* Cuando hacía frío *When it was cold* Durante los meses fríos *During the cold season*	podían dormir en *they could sleep in* podían refugiarse en *they could find refuge in* tenían acceso a *they had access to*	albergues *refuges* centros de acogida *homeless shelters*

Para alimentarse *To feed themselves* Para salir adelante *To get ahead* Para sobrevivir *To survive*	necesitaban *they needed (to)* se veían obligados a *they were forced (to)* tenían que *they had (to)*	buscar en los contenedores *to rummage through bins* pedir limosna *to beg* robar *to steal*

En algunos casos *In some cases* En el peor de los casos *In the worst of cases* Si no tenían más remedio *If they had no other option*	dormían *they slept*	en cajas de cartón *on a cardboard box* en los bancos del metro *on benches in the underground*
	se refugiaban *they found refuge*	bajo un puente *under a bridge* en cajeros automáticos *in ATMs*

La exclusión *Exclusion* La falta de higiene *The lack of hygiene* La pobreza *Poverty* La soledad *Loneliness*	causaba problemas *would cause troubles* llevaba a conflictos *would lead to issues*	de adicciones *addiction* de alcoholismo *alcohol abuse* de drogas *drugs* de salud *health* sociales *social*

Los pobres *The poor people* Estos indigentes *These destitute people*	estaban expuestos al riesgo de *were exposed to the risk of* eran a menudo víctimas de *were often victims of*	humillaciones verbales *verbal humiliation* violencia física *physical violence*

Era, *It was*	y sigue siendo, *and continues to be*	nuestro deber colectivo *our collective duty* nuestra responsabilidad *It was our responsibility*	ayudarles a *to help them to* echarles una mano para *to give them a helping hand*	encontrar una vivienda digna *to find decent accommodation* reinsertarse en la sociedad *to reintegrate into society* salir adelante *to get ahead*

1. Complete the table

Spanish	English
La falta de higiene	
	Drugs
	To give a helping hand
Los indigentes	
	Benches
En el peor de los casos	
En cajas de cartón	

2. Split sentences

Dormían	de violencia física
Causaba los	había más sin techo
Para salir adelante	problemas de drogas
Se refugiaban debajo	nuestro deber
Eran víctimas	en cajas de cartón
Recuerdo que	más joven
Sigue siendo	de puentes
Cuando era	tenían que robar

3. Rewrite the words in bold in the correct order

a. Es nuestra **eisoanrsabpildd**

b. Si no **tnaení** más remedio **orídanm** en los cajeros

c. Podían **gresuiafre** en los centros de **icdogaa**

d. **aeTínn** que buscar en los **rcntnedoesoe**

e. Se veían **gbiladsoo** a pedir limosna

f. **rutaDne** los meses más **íorsf**

g. La **xceusnlió** llevaba a conflictos

h. **ydauAesrl** a reinsertarse en la **ocdeisda**

i. Si no tenían más **meedroi** dormían bajo un **nupete**

4. Complete with the missing words

a. Nuestro deber es echarles ___ mano

b. __ invierno tenían acceso _ centros __ acogida

c. __ algunos casos dormían __ cajas __ cartón

d. __ soledad causaba problemas __ salud mental

e. ____ sobrevivir tenían ___ pedir limosna

f. En __ peor de __ casos __ refugiaban __ cajeros

g. Recuerdo que había más __ techo __ mi barrio

h. Estaban expuestos __ riesgo __ violencia

i. Reinsertarse __ __ sociedad

5. Complete the sentences

a. La _____ de _____ *The lack of hygiene*

b. _____ los meses fríos dormían en los _____ del metro
During cold months, they slept on benches in the underground

c. La mayor parte del tiempo _____ en _____ de cartón
Most of the time, they slept on cardboard boxes

d. Cuando ____ más _____ *When I was younger*

e. Era, y sigue _____, nuestro deber colectivo _____ una mano
It was, and it still is, our collective duty to give them a helping hand

f. En _____ podían _____ en los centros de acogida
In winter they could sleep in homeless shelters

g. Para _____ adelante tenían que pedir _____ *To get ahead, they had to beg*

h. Para _____ se veían _____ a buscar en los _____
To feed themselves, they were forced to rummage through bins

Roberto (26 años, Pinoso, Alicante)

Cuando era más joven, las personas sin hogar eran las personas más pobres de mi ciudad. Muy a menudo, por falta de dinero, dormían en los bancos del metro, en una caja de cartón, en los cajeros o en los pasillos de una estación. Siempre con la esperanza *[hope]* de encontrar algo para comer y vestirse *[to wear]*.

Para sobrevivir, se veían obligados a buscarse la vida, pidiendo limosna o en el peor de los casos, robando. En invierno, durante los meses más duros, solían tener *[they usually had]* acceso a refugios que les ayudaban a encontrar una cama y que les daban comida.

Desafortunadamente, la exclusión a menudo causaba problemas de drogas para algunos de ellos, lo que en ocasiones llevaba a serios problemas de salud. La soledad de las personas sin hogar también podía causar conflictos sociales y trastornos mentales, como la depresión. Algunos de ellos rechazaron *[rejected]* la ayuda externa y no querían mezclarse *[mix]* con otras personas.

Recuerdo que estas personas pobres estaban expuestos cada día al riesgo de humillaciones verbales y a menudo eran víctimas de violencia física. En ese momento yo trabajaba como voluntario en un comedor social de mi barrio y pensé que era mi deber ayudarles a alimentarse dignamente. Era, y sigue siendo, nuestra responsabilidad echarles una mano para reinsertarse en la sociedad.

6. Find the Spanish in the text

a. When I was younger

b. The poorest people in my town

c. Due to lack of money

d. On benches in the underground

e. Always hoping to find

f. In order to survive

g. To find a bed

h. Drug problems

i. Serious health issues

j. Mental illnesses

k. Some of them

l. They rejected external help

m. To mix with other people

n. Often they were victims

o. I remember that

p. A soup kitchen

q. It was, and continues to be...

r. Our responsibility

s. To give them a hand

7. Answer in English

a. What are the four places Roberto remembers seeing homeless people sleep when he was young?

b. What did the homeless have to do in order to cope?

c. What made a difference in the life of the homeless during winter?

d. What are two issues Roberto mentions linked to exclusion?

e. What could loneliness cause for some of them?

f. What type of risks were homeless people exposed to on the street?

g. What's the Spanish for "I used to work"?

8. Complete the translation of the fourth paragraph

I _____ that these poor people were

_____ to the risk of verbal _____ every

day and were often _____ of physical

_____. At the time, I was _____ as a

volunteer in a _____ kitchen in my

_____ and I _____ that it was my

duty to _____ feed themselves with dignity.

It was, _____, our responsibility to lend

them a _____ in order to reintegrate into _____.

THE LANGUAGE GYM

9. Translate into English

a. Se veían obligados a pedir limosna

b. En ese momento, yo trabajaba como voluntario

c. En invierno tenían acceso a los centros de acogida

d. Era, y sigue siendo, nuestro deber colectivo

e. La soledad de las personas sin hogar podía causar conflictos sociales

f. La exclusión causaba problemas de adicciones a las drogas y alcoholismo

g. Cuando hacía frío se veían obligados a dormir en los bancos del metro

h. Para alimentarse necesitaban pedir limosna

i. Los pobres estaban expuestos al riesgo de humiliaciones verbales y violencia física

10. Positive or negative?

a. Dormir en la calle

b. Pasar la noche en una casa y comer dignamente

c. Echar una mano a los sin techo

d. Verse obligado a robar

e. Ayudar a los pobres a alimentarse

f. Morir de frío

g. Refugiarse en las cajas de cartón

h. Tener apoyo de la familia

i. Ser víctima de la violencia física

j. Tener acceso a un albergue

k. Reinsertarse en la sociedad

l. Combatir la adicción

11. Complete with the options provided

Cuando ____ más _____, las personas sin _____ eran las personas más pobres de mi ciudad. Muy a _____, por falta de dinero, dormían en un _____ del metro, en una ____ de cartón o en los _____ de una estación. Para _____ adelante, tenían que pedir _____ o buscar en los contenedores de basura con la _____ de encontrar algo para comer y vestirse. Para _____, se veían _____ a buscarse la vida. En _____, durante los meses más _____, solían tener acceso a refugios, o centros de acogida, que les ayudaban a _____ una cama y comida.

sobrevivir	menudo	limosna	obligados	salir
invierno	encontrar	hogar	era	esperanza
banco	caja	joven	pasillos	duros

12. Translate into Spanish

a. I used to work as a volunteer in a soup kitchen

b. Very often, they slept on a cardboard box

c. It was our responsibility to give them a helping hand

d. Most of the time, they lived on a bench in a park

e. Loneliness could cause troubles of alcohol abuse

f. When it was cold, they could have access to homeless shelters

g. In winter, they could sleep in refuges

h. The homeless were poor people

13. Correct the spelling & grammar errors

a. Es nostra responsabilidad hecharles una mano

b. Podían refugarse en alberges

c. Cuando erra pequeño había menos sin tejos

d. Sigue yendo nuestro deber ayudar a los con techo

e. La falta de hygiene causava problemas

f. Cuanto hacía fredo tenían acceso de albergues

g. Para saltar a delante tenían que pedir limones

Conversación entre amigos

Claudia: Hola Sara. ¿Recuerdas cómo vivían las personas sin hogar en tu ciudad cuando eras más joven?

Sara: Recuerdo que cuando era niña, a menudo había personas sin hogar pidiendo limosna en la entrada del centro comercial. A menudo estaban sucios y olían mal. La mayor parte del tiempo bebían o fumaban.

Claudia: Fuiste voluntaria para una organización benéfica. Cuéntame sobre esta experiencia y el estilo de vida de las personas sin hogar.

Sara: Había dos tipos de personas sin hogar. Para algunos de ellos, la marginación *[marginalisation]* fue una elección. Querían vivir apartados *[separated]* de la sociedad y rechazaron el sistema establecido *[established]*. Para otros, era otra cosa: lo habían perdido todo. Trabajo, casa, familia, amigos... ¡Todo! Para estas personas, era más difícil aceptar su situación.

Claudia: ¿Qué hiciste para ayudarlos?

Sara: Todos los sábados servía comidas a mediodía en un comedor social y luego les ayudaba a rellenar *[fill in]* formularios para darles acceso a alojamiento y alimentación durante el invierno.

Claudia: ¿Qué te pareció esta experiencia?

Sara: Fue una experiencia muy enriquecedora y también fue una lección de humildad. Por una vez en mi vida, me sentí realmente útil porque sabía que realmente ayudaba a esta pobre gente.

14. Find the Spanish for the following expressions

a. When you were younger

b. I remember that

c. There were homeless people

d. They were often dirty and smelt badly

e. They drank or they smoked

f. Tell me about this experience

g. For some of them

h. It was a choice

i. To live away from society

j. They rejected

k. The established system

l. For others, it was something else

m. They had lost everything

n. Employment, home, family, friends

o. It was harder

p. Every Saturday

q. I served food in a soup kitchen

r. To fill in

s. For once in my life

t. I felt really useful

15. Answer in English

a. Where did Sara used to see homeless people in her town when she grew up?

b. How does she remember their physical appearance/state? (2 details)

c. What were they doing most of the time? (2 details)

d. What are the two types of homeless people she describes?

e. What did she used to do every Saturday to help them? (2 details)

f. What did she help them fill in, and why?

g. How did she find this experience? (2 details)

h. How did she feel about helping homeless people? (2 details)

16. Complete the translation from Sara's second and third answer

There _____ two types of _____ people. For some of _____ , marginalisation was a _____ . They _____ to live _____ from society and _____ the _____ system. For _____ , it was something ____: they had _____ everything. _____ , home, family, _____ . _____! For these _____, it was a lot _____ to accept their _____.

Every Saturday I _____ meals at noon in a _____ kitchen and then helped them _____ forms to give them access to _____ and _____ during the winter.

17. Faulty translation: spot the errors in the English translations below and correct

a. Recuerdo que	*I think that*
b. Cuando era niña	*When I was tall*
c. En la entrada	*At the exit*
d. Todos los sábados	*Every Sunday*
e. Servía comidas	*I served drinks*
f. Darles acceso	*Give them drinks*
g. Una lección de humildad	*A lesson in humidity*
h. Acceso a alojamiento	*Access to clothing*
i. Fue muy enriquecedora	*It made me rich*
j. Me sentí	*I realised that*
k. Realmente útil	*Really useless*

18. Translate the following paragraph into Spanish

When I was little, there were often homeless people on my street. To survive, they had to beg or rummage through bins. It was a sad situation. I remember that they were dirty most of the time and they smelt badly too. Some of them drank a lot and they usually slept on a bench in the local park or in the corridors of the train station. Once, I served some food in a soup kitchen to help them. It was a very enriching experience, but it was also very hard. I felt useful and I also made some money donations to help.

19. Answer the following questions to the best of your ability using the Sentence Builder from this unit and the conversation above for support. Then practise with a partner

a. ¿Recuerdas cómo vivían las personas sin hogar en tu ciudad cuando eras más joven?

b. ¿Alguna vez has ayudado a personas sin hogar en tu ciudad? Si es así, ¿qué hiciste para ayudarles?

c ¿Qué te pareció esta experiencia?

d. ¿Qué te gustaría hacer para ayudar a los pobres en el futuro?

20. Challenge: translate the following paragraph into English to the best of your ability

La marginación a veces fue elegida por ciertos individuos que deseaban vivir apartados de la sociedad y fuera del sistema establecido. Desafortunadamente, muy a menudo esta situación llevó a problemas de salud.

Recuerdo que todos los inviernos morían de frío en las calles de mi ciudad personas sin hogar. No tenían los medios económicos para albergarse y alimentarse dignamente.

Estas personas también fueron muy a menudo víctimas de humillaciones verbales y, a veces, incluso de violencia física a plena luz del día.

Era, y sigue siendo, nuestra responsabilidad echarles una mano para reinsertarse en la sociedad.

Key questions

¿Recuerdas cómo vivían las personas sin hogar en tu ciudad cuando eras más joven?	*Do you remember how homeless people lived in your town when you were younger?*
¿Dónde dormían las personas sin hogar durante el invierno?	*Where did the homeless sleep during winter?*
¿Cómo sobrevivían las personas sin techo en las calles?	*How did the homeless survive on the street in those days?*
¿Alguna vez has ayudado a personas sin hogar en tu ciudad? Si es así, ¿cómo?	*Have you ever helped the homeless in your town?If yes, how?*
¿A qué tipo de riesgos estaban expuestos los sin techo en ese momento?	*At what type of risks were the homeless exposed to at that time?*
¿Cómo crees que ayudarás en el futuro?	*How do you think you will help in the future?*

Printed in Great Britain
by Amazon